This is an inspiring book. Alina Schellekes's beautifully rendered case histories concern patients whose symptoms range from hypochondriasis to self-destroying perfectionism to sex addiction, from eating disorders to a sense of inauthenticity or a lack of meaning. In these adults with autistic enclaves and defenses, she documents the prime importance of primitive anxieties, of holes, voids or catastrophic absences in the fabric of the personality, even while she warns against becoming fascinated by these lest the patient's more developed aspects be overlooked. The writing is deeply personal and is enriched by links to literature, theatre and painting, as well as by wide-ranging theoretical scholarship. The book will be indispensable to psychoanalysts, psychotherapists, psychologists and to anyone interested in understanding the human mind, particularly its primitive layers

Maria Rhode, *Professor Emerita of Child Psychotherapy, Tavistock Clinic, London; member of the Association of Child Psychotherapists; child analyst of the British Psychoanalytical Society; recipient of The Frances Tustin Memorial Prize, 1998*

Alina Schellekes illustrates both clinically and theoretically, in a very profound and personal way, the importance of primitive mental states in the construction of psychic life, in both its most vital and most deadening aspects. The integration and synthesis of various theoretical approaches is impressive, and the clinical narratives are evocative, sometimes haunting. The concept of bone-building interpretations will remain as a graphic representation of construction in analysis at a primary and primitive level. This book is inspirational and thought-provoking. A must for a wide range of readers, from lay people to young professionals and seasoned analysts alike.

Patrick Miller, M.D., *training and supervising psychoanalyst of the International Psychoanalytic Association; co-founder and former president of the Société Psychanalytique de Recherche et de Formation-SPRF (Paris)*

The Dread of Falling

The Dread of Falling: Reflections on Primitive Mental States offers a comprehensive and original view of primitive mental states from a psychoanalytic perspective, allowing the reader to understand the nature of these states from developmental, theoretical and clinical vantage points.

The book begins with a review of early mental development and its relevance to the understanding of primitive mental states. Alina Schellekes explores major primary anxieties of being and considers object relations that characterize loose or shattered structures of the self. "The dread of falling" both describes a concrete anxiety prevalent in such states and serves as a metaphor and common thread through the book to portray the deep dread of losing base with one's meaningful objects. Schellekes looks at how, in cases of severe developmental deprivation or late-onset trauma, mental void structures or states of emotional indigestible excess may evolve, creating complex challenges in the analytic process. Schellekes explores various mental survival tactics that are often developed and deployed by patients finding themselves in such extreme cases: omnipotent self-holding defenses, autistic maneuvers, rebirth fantasies and excessive daydreaming. She discusses the quality of analytic presence that is necessary when facing unrepresented mental layers and uncentered states of mind, so as to minimize the risk of toxic states in analysis and of premature terminations.

Including perceptive analyses of literary and fine art works, the book invites the reader on an intellectual and emotional journey through complex mental landscapes of patient and analyst, encompassing profound theoretical understandings and subtle clinical observations.

Alina Schellekes is a Training and Supervising Psychoanalyst of the Israel Psychoanalytic Society; head of the Primitive Mental States advanced track at the Psychoanalytic Program of Psychotherapy, Tel Aviv University; chair of the Frances Tustin Memorial Trust; and recipient in 2006 of the Honorary Mention of Phyllis Meadow Award in New York for excellence in psychoanalytical writing. In 2008, she won the Frances Tustin Memorial Prize; in 2023 the IPA Hayman Prize for Published Work pertaining to Traumatized Children and Adults.

The Routledge Wilfred R. Bion Studies Book Series

The contributions of Wilfred Bion are among the most cited in the analytic literature. Their appeal lies not only in their content and explanatory value, but in their generative potential. Although Bion's training and many of his clinical instincts were deeply rooted in the classical tradition of Melanie Klein, his ideas have a potentially universal appeal. Rather than emphasizing a particular psychic content (e.g., Oedipal conflicts in need of resolution; splits that needed to be healed; preconceived transferences that must be allowed to form and flourish, etc.), he tried to help open and prepare the mind of the analyst (without memory, desire or theoretical preconception) for the encounter with the patient.

Bion's formulations of group mentality and the psychotic and non-psychotic portions of the mind, his theory of thinking and emphasis on facing and articulating the truth of one's existence so that one might truly learn firsthand from one's own experience, his description of psychic development (alpha function and container/contained) and his exploration of O are "non-denominational" concepts that defy relegation to a particular school or orientation of psychoanalysis. Consequently, his ideas have taken root in many places.... and those ideas continue to inform many different branches of psychoanalytic inquiry and interest.[1]

It is with this heritage and its promise for the future developments of psychoanalysis in mind that we present *The Routledge Wilfred Bion Studies Book Series*. This series gathers together newly emerging and continually evolving contributions to psychoanalytic thinking that rest upon Bion's foundational texts and explore and extend the implications of his thought. For a full list of titles in the series, please visit the Routledge website at: https://www.routledge.com/The-Routledge-Wilfred-Bion-Studies-Book-Series/book-series/RWBSBS

Howard B. Levine, MD
Series Editor

---

1   Levine, H.B. and Civitarese, G. (2016). Editors' Preface, The W.R. Bion Tradition, Levine and Civitarese, eds., London: Karnac 2016, p. xxi.

The Dread of Falling

Reflections on Primitive Mental States

Alina Schellekes

R Routledge
Taylor & Francis Group

LONDON AND NEW YORK

Designed cover image: Manuela Antoniu, Falling Through the Still Point (metal and wood, 1986)

First published 2025
by Routledge
4 Park Square, Milton Park, Abingdon, Oxon OX14 4RN

and by Routledge
605 Third Avenue, New York, NY 10158

Routledge is an imprint of the Taylor & Francis Group, an informa business

© 2025 Alina Schellekes

British Library Cataloguing-in-Publication Data
A catalogue record for this book is available from the British Library

Library of Congress Cataloging-in-Publication Data
Names: Schellekes, Alina, author.
Title: The dread of falling : reflections on primitive mental states / Alina Schellekes.
Description: Abingdon, Oxon ; New York, NY : Routledge, 2025. |
Series: The Routledge Wilfred Bion studies book series | Includes bibliographical references and index. |
Identifiers: LCCN 2024051905 (print) | LCCN 2024051906 (ebook) | ISBN 9781032766584 (hardback) | ISBN 9781032758718 (paperback) | ISBN 9781003479482 (ebook)
Subjects: LCSH: Developmental psychology. | Psychoanalysis. | Ethnopsychology.
Classification: LCC BF713 .S325 2025 (print) | LCC BF713 (ebook) | DDC 155.4/6–dc23/eng/20250215
LC record available at https://lccn.loc.gov/2024051905
LC ebook record available at https://lccn.loc.gov/2024051906

ISBN: 978-1-032-76658-4 (hbk)
ISBN: 978-1-032-75871-8 (pbk)
ISBN: 978-1-003-47948-2 (ebk)

DOI: 10.4324/9781003479482

Typeset in Times New Roman
by Taylor & Francis Books

Contents

Foreword: The resolution of absence   viii

DANA AMIR

Introduction   xiv

ALINA SCHELLEKES

1 Early emotional development and primitive mental states: A brief
  perspective   1

2 The dread of falling and dissolving   13

3 When time stood still: Thoughts about time in primitive mental
  states   34

4 Arid mental landscapes and avid cravings for human contact:
  Beckettian and analytic narratives on psychic void and its
  vicissitudes   53

5 Daydreaming and hypochondria: When daydreaming goes wrong
  and hypochondria becomes an autistic retreat   69

6 Sentenced to life: Reflections on trauma and the inability to bear
  vitality, following the movie *Turtles Can Fly*   85

7 Stations along the Via Dolorosa of good enough endings   103

8 Concluding notes: Bone-building interpretations   117

Index   122

Foreword: The resolution of absence

Dana Amir

The great strength of the book you are about to read is the subtle resolution at which it observes a variety of mental phenomena through the prism or the language of primitive mental states. This is a prism that produces a kind of enlargement or amplification, a gentle and painstaking zooming in on processes which reveal themselves in all their complexity and fragility. The chapters fan out, as it were, into a number of unusual mental phenomena: The dread of falling; fragmented time; timelessness; stereotypical time; mental void; hypochondria and excessive daydreaming; what Schellekes calls "being sentenced to life"; the illusion of good enough endings. Let me first consider each chapter's key ideas, in order then to try and bring them together into one statement about the commonalities of the reflections they include.

The opening chapter, "Early Emotional Development and Primitive Mental States," lays the groundwork for the book, offering a kind of "road map" which can be used both as a theoretical exposition in its own right, and as a helpful tool in reading subsequent chapters; in addition, it functions as part of an effort to hone the specific "closeness" required for observing primitive mental states.

The second chapter, "The Dread of Falling and Dissolving," discusses the fright of falling and the defenses that the body and psyche put up against it; that is to say, the chapter deals with forms of collapse into gravity and overcoming gravity as representative of several types of anxieties and the respective manic defenses against them. The case study presents a multitude of relations marked by dense merging, lacking the three-dimensionality and the internal space for processing mental experiences. This universe appears as a flat domain marked by the defense of adhesive identification, which serves as the ultimate barrier to endless fall. Due to the absence of what Schellekes, following André Green and Donald Winnicott, calls "supporting object" (which enables an upright position), the subject transforms into a subject who is being expelled from within themselves, or from the very possibility of interiority. The perspective presented here shows the counterforces to falling – the wish to float or fly – as not merely an omnipotent bid to cope with the dread of falling and collapse but also as expressing a wish to return to an experience of intra-uterine floating, a primary state in which there is no gravity, and where the constraints of time and space are yet to come into play.

The chapter titled "When Time Stood Still" is dedicated to the dimension of time in primitive mental states. More specifically, it looks at three conditionalities of time and timelessness: The experience of fragmented time, which is broken and meaningless; the experience of timelessness, and the ritual and stereotypical relation to time, which results in an experience of static, frozen time. This chapter's central idea is that when time, rather than being a basis or background, turns into an object in its own right, demanding distinct attention, it points at a hidden inner rupture. For Schellekes, time can be a litmus test for specific regions of rupture and the defenses the psyche confronting them puts up. The chapter thus discusses the temporal modalities occurring in the therapeutic hour, and more specifically three modes in which the disruption of the natural mobility between modalities reveals an experience of inner rupture originating in the remote past. The first case presents us with an experience of fragmented time, with Schellekes writing:

> I could appreciate the depth to which she sensed time as fragmented, each moment existing of and by itself, with no sense of connection and continuity from one to the next, or between past, present and future. The way she experienced temporality revealed the depth of her fragmented and perforated experience of herself, as though she were losing her identity in the interval between seconds.

The second case study, by contrast, addresses in Schellekes's analysis

> states when a sense of timelessness is a frequent occurrence (O'Shaughnessy 1992) and where there is a degree of attraction and addiction to the experience, a sort of imprisonment in the moment ... Their nature denies in effect that living is a steady, endless flow of time. This sinking into the present moment disguises a denial both of the past, with all its losses and traumas, and of the future, which carries the inevitability of death.

Unlike fractured time, as in the first case, the timeless present in the second does not embody the ruptures of the past but acts to keep them apart. Again, this close attention to the qualities of time functions as a litmus test to bear out something – but now, rather than pointing at the rupture itself, it shows the resulting scar, which forms thickened skin tissue to protect against the possibility of endless hemorrhaging.

The third modality of time is "frozen, ritualist, stereotypic ... characteristic of psychic states having a prominent autistic encapsulation." In her third vignette, Schellekes illustrates a suspended arrest in time, "in a motionless state, a void of emotional and cognitive movement," alternating with "moments of very concrete speech, extremely repetitive and stereotypical."

Observing the patient's specific experience of time and space, Schellekes illustrates the subtle work of reconstruction of the patient's struggle against the terror of losing continuity and memory, on the one hand, and against the feared encounter with the traumatic sequence of the patient's life, on the other. The pathological temporality set forth in this chapter, in its various modalities, is presented simultaneously as a form of alienation but also as the boldest way of coming close to primitive mental formations which are only registered through their absence.

As will have transpired from Schellekes's writing up to this point, subjects' attitude to time will be contingent on the degree of symbolization or, alternatively, presence of primitive mental states. In more evolved conditions, time is mostly treated as a background or substructure, something which is significantly different in the case of primitive mental states, where it transforms into an object in its own right. In these cases, as a result of a developmental disruption or of a primary developmental arrest, the relations between figure and ground become inverted, transforming factors (such as time) which under different conditions would have functioned as background (thus staying transparent and obvious) into something external, a mental figure. So, what we usually perceive as the substratum, the background for movement and thought, now turns into a developmental objective which requires an entirely different clinical approach. Therapy in cases like the ones presented here does not address breakdown in existing structures but looks to create the very conditions for the development of psychic structures as such. Therefore, time is not an accompanying dimension of existence – rather, a developmental task, an achievement to be achieved: A sense of unbroken time, or of normal temporality, or of non-circular time that must be created. But for this, as Schellekes demonstrates, time must be treated in a different way, or its distinctive status must be recognized both within the patient's narrative and within the therapeutic discourse.

The following chapter, "Arid Mental Landscapes and Avid Cravings for Human Contact," focuses on the psychic void and the defensive strategies against it, namely the manner in which the psyche produces a kind of protective shell that allows avoidance (a-void) of experiences of emotional void and meaninglessness. At one pole of such avoidance of feeling mental emptiness we find the use of what Schellekes calls "envelopes of excitement" and "fantasies of re-birth" – sensory and narcissistic thrills which serve to block out the abyssal experience of the bottomless void, while at the other pole of such avoidance rhythmic, over-controlled and lifeless strategies are mobilized.

One important distinction this chapter elaborates is between "no-thingness" – an empty, passive space that has the potential to become filled with representations – and the phenomenon of the "black hole," whose main feature is its pull into the abyss of non-existence. While no-thingness assumes the existence of an internal container with a clear external wall and a capacity to absorb or take in, namely a three-dimensional structure, even if of a basically passive quality – the black hole, which is typical of the more regressive cases Schellekes pinpoints on either the psychotic or the autistic spectrum, is not felt as a static, passive emptiness but as an "implosive, centripetal pull into the void (Grotstein 1990a)." In these states, structures and rhythms which are normally internalized as stable representations come to serve as autistic objects and hence compensate for the insufficiently developed structure of the self-core. As a result, the periphery of the self undergoes over-development, resulting in a rigid external shell that serves to protect against the dread of disappearance.

The chapter "Daydreaming and Hypochondria" examines the fascinating relations between hypochondria and daydreaming. Here Schellekes proposes that

> the hypochondriac involvement with the body may become so extensive that, at its limit, it can induce autistic-like withdrawals into a world of hypertrophied attention to one's sensations, where daydreaming on disease and deterioration and the ensuing torrent of anxiety become densely intermingled, creating a very painful and detached existence.

She proposes to call this condition (paraphrasing Green's concept of negative hallucination) "negative hypochondria," a state of sparse emotional investment in the living, healthy body. Here Schellekes suggests some ways to relate to possible meanings of the hypochondriac state. Hypochondriac anxiety, for instance, may make a connection – however distorted – to a body that was, in the past, either suspended or denied. Alternatively,

> the imagined pain and suffering that the hypochondriac so extensively fears become, through the person's elaborate attention to physical sensations and imagined scenarios of disease, a sort of psychic retreat (Steiner 1993) into the body, wherein the imagined pain keeps alive the connection with the frustrating invasive object, who often becomes installed into the fantasy of the sick organ.

When the infant's or child's psyche is flooded by unbearable stimulation or painful and erratic experiences, an attachment to pain will develop. As a result, instead of separating from the painful quality of the object's presence and mourning this separation, what emerges is an adhesive attachment to the painful physical and mental qualities associated with this object. Another possibility Schellekes raises is that this hypersensitivity to any physical sign may be a displaced craving for care. Instead of the other satisfying this craving, the craving is displaced into the subject's own concern for their body. In this manner, hypochondria simultaneously serves as a carrier for primitive anxiety and as the way to deny this very anxiety. How then does hypochondria tie in with daydreaming?

Schellekes writes:

> The hypochondriac imagines how every little sign of physical distress and every minor symptom will lead to catastrophic and lethal consequences. Many times, as I have seen with several patients, the imagined scenario includes almost a trance-like state of mind, in which the hypochondriac gets carried away into an elaborate fantasy of how they (or a very close person) will be diagnosed as gravely ill, how their organs will deteriorate, how days and nights will be spent in pain and anguish while undergoing medical treatments and prolonged hospitalizations, how lonely and frightful such states will be experienced as. These daydreamed narratives, when employed excessively, acquire autistic features, as the hypochondriac sinks into a world governed by sensations, getting more and more detached from their surroundings and wailing/lamenting the miserable imagined existence that will befall them.

Schellekes suggests that the hypochondriac person's thought processes consist of mixed layers, some of which are saturated by masochistic fantasies made up of symbols, while in others the imagining of body feelings and the immersion in them produce a kind of autistic enclave bereft of any symbolic activity. Here, too, the prism of primitive mental states makes a unique contribution, in an opposite manner to the established thinking about daydreaming as a version of the oedipal fantasy concerning the ideal romantic family. For Schellekes, daydreams of this kind are of a much more primitive order; in fact, they are regressive shells allowing withdrawal into imaginary realms. They are a kind of "daydreaming envelope" compensating for the absence, or for a failure, of the basic functions of containment.

The next chapter, "Sentenced to Life," discusses patients who are unable to tolerate the encounter with their own vitality or that of the other – a vitality which for them is an overwhelming, aggressive, and undigestible experiential excess. In these cases, the degree of vitality and connection – whether within the patients themselves or between them and the analyst – must be very precisely calibrated and with great gentleness because otherwise it might lead to what Schellekes calls "toxemia of therapy," when the emotional climate in the room – a function of the therapist's vitality and the degree of proximity to the patient – is beyond what the patient can take in and process. This leads the patient to experience the therapy as disastrous, a catastrophic inundation. Offering a fresh understanding of the topic of negative therapeutic reaction, this chapter, too, rather than stress the developmentally more advanced version of resistance, resulting from a well-defined personality structure and its associated conflicts, focuses on the primitive states in which the living other produces a dangerous congestion threatening the subject's fragile boundaries and their very ability to contain.

The chapter "Stations along the Via Dolorosa of Good Enough Endings" focuses on the partly realistic, partly illusional concept of a "good-enough ending" in analysis/therapy. Schellekes addresses in this important chapter some of the obstacles that interfere with achieving this yearned-for goal, leading to endings that are far from the illusion, that many of us hold, of the good-enough termination and that are reported by many therapists and analysts. Thus, she dwells on characteristics, obstacles, blockages, dreads within the analyst and in the space in-between, linking in a unique way the analytic set of beliefs, myths, and thoughts towards "good-enough" endings with the perception of beginning.

Finally, Schellekes's concluding notes focus on what she calls "Bone-building interpretations." In the absence of a holding center, "uncentered mental states," which are analogous to "the physiological state of a baby who is still incapable of sitting or holding itself upright," cause disintegrating primary anxieties, inescapable emptiness, and the danger of fragmentation.

These primitive mental states obviously necessitate the stable, containing and holding presence of the analyst and the analytic setting. The qualities of this presence create a fundamental preliminary prop analogous to a plaster cast – a passive device required when dealing with physical fractures. However, this stable, containing, and holding presence is necessary but not sufficient in many of the extreme states addressed in this book, which require the analyst's highly active presence, a kind capable of facilitating the growth of a solid psychic bone structure. In extreme states, in which a psychic support pillar, rather than being broken down, has failed to emerge – what is required, according to Schellekes, is a presence that is also bone-building – an active presence that is not merely a passive external cast but also functions as a platform for developing the lacking internal core.

Introduction

Alina Schellekes

Dear Readers,

I would like to try and give you some idea of the processes that went into the making of this book. It is a collection of articles and papers I wrote between 2007 and 2023. Almost all of them touch upon what tends to be called "primitive mental states," a topic with which I have been deeply and enduringly fascinated. Here I will dwell upon some emotional and professional moments that occurred as I was writing and gathering these chapters.

To begin with, some personal history: During my childhood and adolescence in Bucharest, Romania, I witnessed, and participated in, some extremely difficult family situations that arose under the country's communist and totalitarian regime. Inside me I accumulated many complex experiences which affected how I developed. This same regime, which massively constrained our private lives, also generated an extensive and very rich educational system which especially emphasized the sciences. In this cultural climate, I learned a lot as well. I developed a passion for physics and chemistry and did very well at both. These subjects fascinated me as they offered the possibility of learning about the workings of the outside world. This passion was also greatly influenced by some formative figures that crossed my path. But when, in adolescence, I encountered some educational professionals whose love of teaching was dwarfed by harsh personality features, my enthusiasm for the sciences abated.

These difficult experiences, together with my long-standing wish to learn about the human psyche, led me, in early adolescence, away from the physical study of the world and towards a new desire to deepen my understanding of psychic processes. In those years, the study of psychology in Romania was no longer possible: Faculties of psychology closed and were replaced by departments dedicated to various Marxist disciplines. Reading material related to psychology was hard to come by. Still, the hungrier I grew for texts, the more roundabout ways to professional literature in English I found – especially, but not only, to Freud's work. I read these underground publications eagerly. And so, when I was around 15 or 16, it became clear to me that I wanted to become a psychologist.

When, at age 16, I immigrated to Israel with part of my family, a much larger choice of books became available to me, allowing me to read to my heart's delight. Three years later, I was so excited to enroll in the Department of Psychology at Tel Aviv University. Now I had many possibilities to gain clinical experience, and curiosity together with my own psychic needs drove me to the most challenging places – like the closed ward for autistic young people at Abarbanel Psychiatric Hospital, where I did two years of voluntary work. It was there that I met some of the most difficult cases of autism I was to encounter in my life. I visited the ward once or twice weekly and worked with a girl who was hospitalized there. Since I received no supervision, I had to rely on my own insight and intuition. These were formative years in my professional development. I had to think for myself about the unthinkable, to make sense of sounds, scenes and senseless motions and dig deep within myself for something that would allow me to connect with the girl and touch her psychic texture. At the same time, I was also working with a girl suffering from elective mutism, whom I accompanied over the course of one year.

These two initial experiences generated a dramatic layer of contact with difficult, non-verbal psychic strata. In this same period, I also volunteered at a meeting place for post-psychotic patients at the Brill Mental Health Center, Ramat Chen, Tel Aviv. Here, too, I became acquainted with some very serious cases. Eventually, Ramat Chen became the place where I ended up working for nearly four decades. As part of my work in this context, I was also employed at the clinic's day-care department, then under the direction of the extremely erudite late Prof. Yehuda Fried, who inspired me to further develop my knowledge concerning psychosis and highly regressive states. In spite of the fact that these experiences were my very first and unripe ones, to be followed by many years of training and work, I perceive these early years as imbued with the intensity of first love, of formative experiences which deeply engraved themselves onto my psyche.

In time, as I continued developing professionally and personally, I noticed how it was mainly primitive mental states that magnetized me, ones I recognized from my own early psychic pains, in my readings, as well as in the patients with whom I worked.

While I was training in various programs and doing my clinical work, I began to pay attention to certain phenomena in my own life. I will only mention one recurrent dream in which a porcelain doll tumbles down the stairs, her legs and arms breaking. Revealing a deep psychic layer, this dream preoccupied me greatly. And so, it and other similar experiences, together with my above-mentioned work, induced me to find out more about parts of the personality with an autistic or primitive quality. This led me, in the late 1980s, to the work of Frances Tustin, which opened up an exciting new world, both experientially and intellectually, and introduced me to other thinkers who had tried to find their way into the kind of processes that interested me. So, for instance, the writings of Judith Mitrani left a deep impression, as did those of James Grotstein, Maria Rhode, Suzanne Maiello, André Green, in addition to many other French and Italian psychoanalytic writers. Eugenio Gaddini's thinking had a special impact, in that it was remarkably deep and creative regarding primitive developmental phases and the various pathologies associated with disruptions in this development.

Over the years, much of my psychotherapeutic and psychoanalytical work, whether directly with patients or through my supervisees, has been with people with extremely regressive personality cores, even if they managed to function well enough in various other domains of their lives. When I finished my own analytic training in 2003, I began to write about these things. This process was accelerated thanks to my work in the Psychoanalytic Psychotherapy Program, Faculty of Medicine, at Tel Aviv University, and as a result of my initiative to open a track for advanced studies on primitive mental states.[1] I have been leading this track for the past eighteen years, with enormous help from a team of teachers and supervisors whose professionalism and dedication have been extraordinary.

Over the course of the last twenty-five years, I have been writing and lecturing on a cluster of topics that all relate, directly or indirectly, to primitive mental states. The articles and papers I selected for this book do not appear in the chronological order of their writing or publication. I preferred to present them here in regard to their content, as I saw fit. The original date of writing is mentioned at the beginning of each chapter. Since I chose to leave the texts as they were, readers might come across some paragraphs they have already read elsewhere in the book. For me, this functions as a through-line that links the subjects I discuss, and is the reason why I left these repetitions untouched.

I would like to thank a number of people, encountering whom has affected my very being, the person I have become, my thinking and my professional understanding. To start with, I extend my gratitude to my patients and supervisees. This book would not have come into being had I not met them, learned from them, been on the receiving end of their trust and their willingness to undergo the therapeutic process, the supervision or the analysis, long periods of often painful and taxing moments, search and change. I would never have written the papers included in this book without being part of a daily struggle for psychic survival, theirs and mine, in often unbearable conditions, or without their compassion where I made mistakes and their forbearance of sometimes prolonged states of unknowing.

Also, I thank all my former colleagues at the Brill Mental Health Center, Ramat Chen, Tel Aviv as well as all the students I taught and trained there. I am grateful for the opportunity I was granted by those in charge to work so intensively with very gifted practitioners in a generous space of engagement. This has been an indispensable contribution to my professional development.

From the very depths of my heart – my gratitude to Prof. Dana Amir for her foreword to this book, written with great sensitivity, profound wisdom and generosity.

None of the chapters in this book would have been written had I not lived the life I have lived and become what I have become. This includes the impact of the many writers I have read and the personal, intellectually and emotionally enriching interactions with people I encountered at meaningful junctures along my way: The late Marcela Onitiu, Dr. Manuela Antoniu, Florin Jacob Brickman, the late Dr. Shai Schellekes, Dr. Andre Draznin, Dr. Judith Mitrani, the late Prof. Yehuda Fried, Dr. Aviva Yahav, Prof. Emanuel Berman, Ruth Levitt, the late Dr. Shifra Arazi, Naama Keinan, Batya Frizel, Dr. Zvi Segal, Prof. Moshe Halevi Spero, Yoel Miller, Edith Barak-Melamed, Judith Triest, Gila Horesh, Mindy Beigel, Ethel Tabachnik, the late Frédérique Tecucianu. I owe each of you my most heartfelt thanks. Each of you, I trust, knows very well what part you have played in my life, so I will allow myself to not spell it out here.

I would like to thank everyone from the Israel Psychoanalytic Society who contributed immensely to my professional development – my teachers and supervisors, my students and supervisees.

I would like to thank as well the heads of the Psychoanalytic Psychotherapy Program at Tel Aviv University's Faculty of Medicine: Dr. Michel Granek, Prof. Shlomo Mendelovich, Dr. Boaz Shalgi, Prof. Merav Roth and Dr. Shlomit Yadlin-Gadot, all of whom have enabled, each in their own way during the past 21 years, a great space for activity, thinking and teaching. My involvement in the program has added much to my professional activity and made a substantial contribution to my development and my ability to write these chapters.

Eighteen years of teaching, training and management in the track for primitive mental states gave me the opportunity to meet and work with around 200 students and with a large team of teachers and supervisors. This encounter with both students and staff members came to constitute a nourishing and sustaining home, emotionally and professionally. I owe you all many thanks.

Here I would like to mention also the reading group formed with some of the staff (Yoel Miller, Anat Telerant, Alona Timor, Hanna Wakstein, Tessa Zadok, Irit Hameiri Valdarski). We have been meeting once every two or three weeks for the past eighteen years to read particularly challenging professional texts, to think together and communicate by means of the rich and exquisite intellectual, emotional and sensory fabric that has spun itself between us.

I wish to express my deep gratitude to Dr. Howard Levine, who suggested the publication of this book in its English version and adopted this project with his sharp mind, crystal-clear thinking, generous heart and endless passion for expanding psychoanalytic knowledge. Many thanks for enabling such a free space for play and reflection.

My appreciation and gratefulness for all the work that has been done by the Routledge team: Zoë Meyer (editor), Deepika Batra (editorial assistant), Jana Craddock (editorial assistant), Sarah Sibley (copyeditor), Sophie Dixon-Dash (production editor) and Mat Willis (cover designer) to bring this book to its final production and for all the patience, help and support that I have received along this process.

My special thanks and gratitude to Dr. Manuela Antoniu, my dearest friend, who has been a central pillar in my life, since adolescence, and who proofread this book, with her exquisite mind and knowledge of the English language and who has also contributed her work for the cover of this book.

My final and special thanks – well beyond my ability to put into words – is to my children, Inbal Faygenboim (Schellekes) and Nadav Schellekes, who made me the mother (and subsequently grandmother) I have become, and who, with their precious and particular souls, gifted me with the most significant years of my life. Even though they were not active partners in the writing of this book, their presence and that of their partners, Alon Faygenboim and Sagi Kill-Schellekes, is inextricably part of the emotional texture that breathes and flows through each and every line of this book.

Alina (Brickman) Schellekes, 2024

Note

1 The first stages of conception of this new track occurred in a steering committee with Naama Keinan and the late Moshe Landau.

Chapter 1

Early emotional development and primitive mental states

A brief perspective[1]

> *I approach and ye vanish away,*
> *I grasp you, and ye are gone;*
> *But ever by night and by day,*
> *The melody soundeth on.*
> —Henry Wadsworth Longfellow, "Fata Morgana" (1883, p. 228)

Some time ago, a colleague asked me: Why is there a need for a special program of studies on primitive mental states? I do not remember the exact answer I gave her, but it was by means of an analogy: I recalled a prior event when I had to locate on an internet map of Paris a hotel situated very centrally in the city, seemingly within reach of everything. However, when I used the zoom-in feature of the map, the hotel now appeared as if in totally different surroundings, far away from what initially had seemed to be in close proximity to it. The whole perspective on the hotel changed, and its environs now looked much richer in details and colors. I told my colleague that in a comparable way I perceive the need to have a place where one can zoom in, closer and closer, in an attempt to understand and work with what we call primitive/primary. In a more circumscribed sense, this is also my goal in this chapter.

Many psychoanalytic theories touch on this topic, one way or another, but the perspective on, and the understanding of, the topic is completely different when one zooms in, each time a little more, and discovers new aspects and nuances that could not be perceived when the view was from a broad and rather distant angle.

One could say that this zoom-in process also has the qualities of the *fata morgana* phenomenon; a fascination with an enigmatic figure which fades away, the closer one approaches it. I regard this fascination as a sine qua non of the urge to study the origins of our mind, something that is, ultimately, unknowable or that at any rate cannot be represented.[2]

If we now zoom in a little on the term "primitive," we can see that what may at first glance appear to be a clear concept can be deconstructed into various meanings, and that each meaning can be further zoomed in on, down to the level of knowledge and understanding of which we are capable at

DOI: 10.4324/9781003479482-1

present. For example, one can choose to refer to the unorganized or dis-organized aspects of mental functioning, and consequently to levels of per-sonality organization; or, one can speak of topographic considerations, so that what is unconscious becomes equivalent to what is primitive; or else one can speak of the term "primitive" as designating the early/primary aspects of development, the origin of any certain behavior. And, last but not least, one can employ the term to speak of the fundamental, elemental parts in oneself, as when one speaks of the infant/child in the adult, in the psychological sense of the word (Grotstein 1997).

These various connotations of the term "primitive" overlap to a great extent, but it is still worthwhile trying to reflect on the particular connotation we are talking about, especially since there is often great confusion, both clinically and theoretically. For instance, when one speaks of the infantile part in an adult patient, one might, sometimes wrongly, assume that this part reflects exactly the child or infant this adult once was, or one may assume that the characteristics of a regressed state are a duplication of an identical state in one's early develop-ment, which, again, is not necessarily the case. Though the infantile parts in one's personality are not an exact duplication of the infant's mind, we generally tend to search back into one's origins of development, as far as we can get to, even if we keep in mind, as I suggest, that the *fata morgana* phenomenon is ever present and that the best we can get to is, to a great extent, a reconstruction made by adult minds of what it is to be an infant.

In the psychoanalytic realm of understanding, two major approaches have helped us so far in the endeavor to apprehend the elusive nature of the infant's mind: One is psychoanalytic thinking, based on clinical experience and theorization of this experience; the other is based on psychoanalytic interpretations of infant observations and developmental studies.

On the theoretical level, if we think of the Freudian baby, the Kleinian baby, the Winnicottian baby, the intersubjective baby, to name just a few, we encounter completely different babies. Two main trends are evident in the theoretical discussion of the infant's mind: One which stresses the concept of primary narcissism at the beginning of emotional development and perceives the infant in a fused state of mind with the object in which undifferentiation from, and merger with, the object are the main characteristics of this very early phase. The relevant proponents of this view are Freud (1914), Spitz (1959), Mahler (1968), Winnicott (1949, 1960), Gaddini (1976) and, partially, Tustin (1981). A different perspective is proposed by all who view the infant mind as having its separate existence and crude awareness of the object from the very beginning of life, such as Klein (1928, 1940) and her followers, Bowlby (1980, 1988), Stern (1985), and Trevarthen (1980). These latter wri-ters are of course aware of the immaturity of the infant mind but emphasize the infant's rudimentary sense of separateness from the object and its capacity to relate to, and communicate with, the primary objects right from the beginning of life. In other words, the main issue at stake between these two opposing views is to what extent the other is already present in the subject. What is the degree of awareness of the subjectivity of the other? And to what extent is an initial merger with the object required in order to develop a healthy sense of self? These differences are not only relevant theoretically or developmentally but also have a dramatic impact on the clinical situation, on the understanding of, and reaction to, the transference.

Another axis from which to look at the primitive nature of the infant's mind is through Bion's rich thinking. In his early writings, Bion (1962, 1965) distinguished between primitive mental states characteristic of the beginning of life and bizarre psychotic ones, in which transformations in hallucinosis and reversal of alpha functions occur. In other words, "he distinguished between the continuity inherent in the axis of primitivity-maturity, where primitivity is associated with immaturity, and the discontinuity between the primitive and the bizarre, where a deformative alteration of the mind and its products occurs" (Grotstein 1997). In his last writings, Bion focused less on the psychotic parts of the personality and more on those aspects in us which have very archaic origins and are vestiges of prenatal phenomena, either of a personal origin or pertaining to universal knowledge.

On a rather broad level, Bion claimed that the breast and most objects that are to be discovered are already present in the infant's mind as preconceptions awaiting their realization in actual experience, in order to become conceptions in reality. In other words, our knowledge is older than the knower, or, in more clinical terms, one may speak of phantasies that exist prior to the meeting with the object. These phantasies constitute what can be called "universal (collective) memory preconceptions" (Grotstein 1997), which Bion poetically termed "memoirs of the future" (Bion 1975, 1977, 1979), meaning that there are some prehistoric memories in our unconscious anticipating the future of our development.[3] On a more specific and personal level, in these last writings, Bion speaks of the impact that prenatal sensations may have on the later development of personality. For example, in the amniotic fluid medium of the womb, the fetus experiences oscillations, noises and sounds that come from the mother's digestive system, the mother's rhythmic heart rate, the sound of the mother's voice or that of others, alternating with silence, sounds and noises in the surrounding environment. These sounds and noises may all give the fetus a proto-experience of presence and absence of the object, which forms the basis of a prenatal sensuous object, named the "sound object" by Suzanne Maiello (1995).

The fetus also experiences the "osmotic pressure" of the mother's mental states (Rosenfeld 1987, p. 276) and various other visual, auditory, olfactory and kinesthetic occurrences. These primary sensations in the uterus may create the first germs of ideas/feelings, which become "proto-emotions," rudiments of a sensual womb object. These proto-emotions together with the "sound object," also connected with a preconception of the breast, may be the precursors of the postnatal maternal inner object.

The more disturbing proto-emotions are characterized by "sub-thalamic terror," a kind of fear which is not controlled by the higher levels of the mind and which therefore has no mental meaning (Bianchedi et al. 2002). One can even say that the relations the fetus establishes with the interior of the mother's body, including with the placenta and the umbilical cord,[4] become the forerunners of relations established after birth (Osterweil 2002; Piontelli 1992) and thus constitute a sort of primary introject, laying the basis for a "prenatal nucleus of the ego" (Raskovsky 1956).

The vestiges of these prenatal, as well as birth, experiences might be stored at a somatic or sensation-based level as body memories (Mitrani 1996, 1997) that can become reactivated in later life in situations which mimic some sensorial or emotional features of the initial prenatal situation. One of the situations in which these archaic, unmentalized states of mind are recreated and enacted is the transference situation, where the setting's inherent containing features as well the analyst's mind/womb enable these "embryonic states of mind" to be born, communicated and eventually understood (Mitrani 1997). For example, the analyst is often treated as a placental object, both receiving the fetus's poisonous materials and transferring to the fetus oxygen and nourishment. This reciprocal process was viewed by Bion as a prenatal precursor of projective identification. We can frequently be aware of the large gamut of affects that characterize the patient's perceptions of the analyst and the analytic room as either holding and containing or as suffocating and limiting, all of which can be traced to similar prenatal or infancy experiences (Ploye 2006).

A fascinating development in post-Bionian thinking has been the extensive discussion of patients who can be characterized by negative identifications, whose central experience is that of non-being, a sort of dead-void existence in which emotional birth has never really happened. One may describe these patients as being frozen in a static time, with no affective movement, waiting for life to start while passively opposing any movement that might bring about change. In these "dead patients" (resonating with Green's "dead mother" concept (Green 1980)), there is a massive inversion of holding and containing, an evacuation of the child's psyche so as to contain a spilling over and invasive mother/object. In other words, the central basic unconscious phantasy becomes that of an existence being hollowed out, a sort of "psychic abortion" (Gonzalez 2010).

Some (Wilheim 2010) have gone so far as to speak of a "cellular memory," a sort of mnemic trace of phantasies that accompanied the moment of conception. In this line of thinking, when the coming together of the two cells had the implied meaning that this act should never have happened, this traumatic pre-conception phantasy becomes stored as a primitive sub-representation of something which had to fall or to be aborted. The ensuing catastrophic feeling might accompany any new situation which promotes growth or is linked with the meaning of conception, birth and development.

The catastrophic anxiety described above becomes activated by any "cae-sura,"[5] by any coming together or by any potential change that is encoun-tered, eventually leading to attacks on whatever is perceived as a meeting of two minds, like those of the analyst's and the patient's. In other words, what used to be called negative therapeutic reaction or attacks on the analytical link can be understood as resulting from the surfacing of "very early prenatal traumatic experiences sensorially imprinted on the … fetus when it felt the threat of being annihilated, aborted or destroyed" (Wilheim 2010). Wilheim's thinking is fascinating, but keeping in mind the reservations I expressed at the beginning of this chapter, we can wonder to what extent the anxiety experi-enced towards any link and the attack on any link in adult life are identical to the texture of the prenatal experience and to what extent the cellular memory invoked by Wilheim is indeed a sensual memory preceding the coming into being of images and representations. Or, we can wonder whether this concept incorporates a retroactive projection of a phantasy, an adult-level-of-thinking phantasy towards the beginning of development.

An additional fascinating way of thinking about anxiety/dread of change and progress, and which connects this anxiety to the beginning of develop-ment, is that of Gaddini and Grotstein. Eugenio Gaddini, one of the most original and important Italian psychoanalysts, conceived of early develop-ment as a phase of total merging between baby and mother. According to his understanding, the first weeks in the infant's development are characterized by a lack of separateness, a magical, omnipotent existence within which the infant experiences itself as a huge creature, since everything that it experiences through its senses is perceived as part of itself and consequently, through the principle of assimilation, magnifies and contributes to the sense of a huge and total self (Gaddini 1976). So far, Gaddini's thinking is similar to Winnicott's, the latter suggesting that the mind's state at the beginning of development lacks differentiation between self and object, the object being perceived as part of the self, magically created by the self, of course as long as the object presents itself to the subject at the right time. But here Gaddini and Winnicott part company. According to Winnicott, as long as the object is totally adap-ted to the infant at the beginning of development, and only later on becomes partially adapted (good enough), the baby can experience a continuity of being without any "unthinkable anxieties" (Winnicott 1962), which are prone to appear when the object's dedication and adaptation to the baby's needs are lacking. Thus, in normal development, depending on the object's adaptation, the Winnicottian infant can experience a smooth transition towards realiza-tion of separateness.

In contrast to Winnicott, Gaddini viewed the early phases of development in a less romantic way. According to him, the more the baby advances in its development, the more it acquires various sensual experiences, various memory traces which enable the baby to gradually realize, albeit in a very basic and simplistic way, that it is separate from the object. The beginning of this understanding marks the beginning of a huge developmental shattering that accompanies every human being, even in normal development. What happens at this stage is the collapse of totality, the collapse of the experience of having an omnipotent self. During this developmental rupture, the infant starts to realize not only that it is not omnipotent and not infinite but that it is actually a small creature, with clear boundaries and limited abilities, totally dependent on the object and on the surrounding world. Due to this new evolving understanding, the infant experiences itself as very small and weak, vulnerable and prone to being injured. This realization is simultaneously accompanied by catastrophic anxiety, the result of the huge gap between the experience of a total self, which now is fractured and collapses, and the experience of a limited, small and vulnerable self. From now on, this small self will worry about its wholeness/entirety, an anxiety which Gaddini named "loss-of-self anxiety" – that is, the anxiety of losing that small self which survived the realization of separateness and of the loss of totality of self.

This loss-of-self anxiety protects the developing self so that it will not experience again the catastrophic anxiety that it has already experienced. The loss-of-self anxiety is prone to be aroused time and again during the various stages of development, at every stage of separateness, at every stage during which the developing infant is supposed to feel more and more able to be separate from the object. If the first realization of separateness was accompanied by particularly intense catastrophic anxiety, and if the resulting experience of the self is of a very vulnerable self, then there is great danger that any change towards separateness will echo the original catastrophic anxiety, and the infant will experience a loss of its now small and vulnerable self. Facing this anxiety, the infant might develop various omnipotent defenses, including psychosomatic symptoms, that will enable it both to express the renewed anxiety and to put in train a regressive state, under the defensive omnipotent control of the self. In such regressive states, a return to an earlier and familiar state of merging with the object is facilitated by the symptom and by the magical omnipotent thinking activated by it.

I have expanded this description of Gaddini's thinking because of its originality and contribution not only to the understanding of early emotional development and the anxieties that accompany this phase of development but also because of the light it throws on the deep anxieties we witness that accompany any developmental change, even in adulthood, including developmental changes during therapy or analysis. In Gaddini's language, the anxiety of change and growth, the "integration anxiety," may be experienced as so threatening that the self will "prefer" to generate acts of fragmentation and regression, under its own control – that is, to generate states of non-integration. Although these states of fragmentation also arouse anxiety, because any state of fragmentation is dreadfully frightening and arouses non-integration anxiety, this fragmentation is experienced nevertheless as more bearable due to its being under the self's omnipotent and defensive control and to its being a return to an archaic, more familiar state.

This thinking is highly relevant in clinical states wherein we witness the patient's difficulty in experiencing the analyst's separateness, in all its varieties and nuances. Facing any signs of the analyst's separateness and at any stage which encompasses representations of separateness and change, the patient might experience a loss-of-self anxiety that echoes the archaic catastrophic anxiety experienced when the infant first realized its separateness from the object. In such states, a defensive regression might occur, coupled with massive resistance to change. This line of thought is of course relevant when we try to understand phenomena such as negative therapeutic reactions.

Grotstein (2010) developed this idea even more when stating that the negative therapeutic reaction can be understood along completely different lines if one takes into account that the patient's resistance to change speaks "a voice from the crypt," the voice of that infant/child who was "cast away" in early life and who, by "haunting the analytic domain, pleads for acknowledgement, rescue, justice and redemption" (see also Schellekes 2009). This voice, in Grotstein's understanding, is the voice of the baby within the adult that pleads to be heard and to make present its primary developmental needs that in the adult's distant past had been frustrated and have not yet received their due and fundamental utterance in the web of object relations. In this sense, the transference becomes not only a medium for voicing this archaic silenced voice but also enables the growth of a potential texture of object relations that is different from the one experienced at the beginning of one's life.

After having described, even if briefly, some of the enactments in the psychoanalytic encounter that express and are modulated by prenatal or infancy-related experiences, I wish to emphasize again that regression and transference are never an exact duplication of an early experience, since much is added, accumulated and distorted during one's development, so that what we see at a given moment in therapy or analysis is but a gross approximation of the initial situation.[6] Therefore, much caution is needed when we face and interpret the transference. Moreover, transference interpretations can frequently become a medium we sometimes stick to abusively/rigidly if not adhesively, as they provide so often an illusion of knowledge about one's most primitive, unknown-unknowable layers of mind.[7]

A very different shift in the paradigm of studying and understanding early emotional development occurred through the growing emphasis on infant observations in the first months and years of development (Bick (1964) and her followers (Briggs 2002)). Both the Tavistock model and Ester Bick's observational studies, by focusing their observations in the first months and years of life, have widely expanded our knowledge of infant development. In particular, they stress the importance of basing this knowledge on clinical observation of infants in their environment rather than extrapolating, often retroactively, from theory or analytic practice.

Though the knowledge accumulated through these observations and its clinical implications are vast, I would like to focus on an additional and extremely important shift in understanding early emotional development, enabled by integrated knowledge from developmental studies, neurophysiology, analytic practice and fetus observations from a very early age of gestation. Daniel Stern's pioneering work and Mauro Mancia's writings have contributed significantly to our understanding of the formation of the earliest sense of self, one which is mainly preverbal and pre-representational. Stern (1985, 2002) described the infant's development of a basic sense of self as proceeding in a series of overlapping and interdependent layers, all interpersonally determined, which eventually create a core affective nucleus. By means of "perceptive amodality"– that is, of the ability to integrate sensations received from one channel into a sensation that makes use of other sensory channels, the infant gradually integrates its experiences and creates very rudimentary representations of itself in relation to others. During the first years of life, six senses of self[8] are acquired which form the basis of what will accompany later development, even if in a much more mature and sophisticated sense.

Mancia (1981, 1988, 1989) expanded Stern's ideas, especially in terms of focusing on the prenatal roots of emotional development. According to Mancia, all the various stimuli that the fetus receives through its various sensory channels, from both its own body and that of its mother's, have their rhythm and constancy, characteristics which become the basis of a first primordial sense of time and of object presence. These various stimuli are colored by their respective pleasant or unpleasant tone, thus becoming what can be called "protomental experiences." All these protomental experiences are integrated by means of the perceptive amodality principle and by the psychic work taking place during active sleep periods, eventually forming what Mancia called a "protomental nucleus of activity" or a "somato-psy-chical self,"[9] to be further developed during growth processes. Mancia's conclusions imply that this pre-representational self is endowed with basic memory abilities and is capable of extending a certain continuity between pre- and post-natal experiences. Mancia's "pre-representational self" reminds one of Bion's "pre-conceptions" – both authors pointing to "active elements of the prenatal self that prepare the newborn baby for its encounter with real objects" (Mancia 1989).

This idea, that birth does not necessarily create a caesura, a rupture in emotional development, but that there is a continuum between pre- and post-natal behavior is central in Piontelli's writings (Piontelli 1986, 1992, 2002, 2010). Piontelli astutely describes patterns of behavior and of relating to the uterine space, including the placenta, that act as forerunners of early behavior and constitute primary roots of object relations. However, in her later writings, Piontelli emphasized and cautioned that these pre-natal "facts" that we have been used to seeing as present in all phantasies and play before the age of four or five have become mixed up with many additions and aftermaths from later periods of development. Although pre-natal factors have been identified, their later presence is completely different from the linear, direct and all-encompassing version of their past. Thus, the prenatal life has lost its factual realistic quality and has become colored more and more by emotions and phantasies related to the prenatal phase. In some cases, the prenatal life has become idealized, while in others it has been imbued with persecutory and claustrophobic anxieties.

If we zoom out now and adopt a bird's eye view of the various prisms through which I chose to talk in this chapter about early emotional development, we can see that each prism is heavily colored, and even distorted, by one's "basic assumptions" on the subject. In my view, the many writings that I have discussed, each influenced by the theory through which it has been crystallized, help us in our attempt to get as close as possible to observing and understanding the origins of human behavioral patterns and constitutional traits that are active long before birth. I hope that this short introduction takes us at least one step further in what sometimes seems our *fata morgana*-like search to understand the origins of our mind.

Notes

1 A shorter version of this chapter was published in Portuguese in: Schellekes, A. (2012). Desenvolvimento emocional precoce e estados mentais primitivos: um breve panorama. *Revista Brasileira de Psicanálise, 46*(4): 187–195. This chapter is included here thanks to the permission granted by the *British Journal of Psychotherapy*, where it was published in a slightly different version in 2021: Schellekes, A. (2021). Early emotional development and primitive mental states – A brief perspective. *British Journal of Psychotherapy, 37*(4): 594–605.

2 When we think in linear terms, the formation of a representation is based on the ability to experience sequences of discrete events. But when we speak of the origin of what each of us has become as a particular human being, we actually speak of an unknowable and unrepresentable source, which may manifest itself through intermediaries or negations. Such an intermediary is an iconic image whose origin is inaccessible to cognition, and thus aniconic; see Eric Rhode (2003) for a thorough discussion of the term "aniconic."

3 From a different theoretical perspective, relevant here is Jung's concept of the "collective unconscious": " ... in addition to our immediate consciousness, which is of a thoroughly personal nature and which we believe to be the only empirical psyche (even if we tack on the personal unconscious as an appendix), there exists a second psychic system of a collective, universal, and impersonal nature which is identical in all individuals. This collective unconscious does not develop individually but is inherited. It consists of pre-existent forms, the archetypes, which can only become conscious secondarily and which give definite form to certain psychic contents" (Jung 1936).

My gratitude to the late Frédérique Tecucianu for reminding me of Jung's relevance for the present discussion.

4 The intimate relation that the fetus establishes with the placenta is echoed among the Mynyanka people of West Africa, who perceive the placenta as a sort of alter ego of the newborn and whose burial ritual includes burial of a jar containing the placenta (Rhode 2003). Analogously, the fetus's relationship with the umbilical cord, as enfolding and protecting versus entangling and inhibiting, is projected into the image of the snake, which in many civilizations is highly loaded with emotional

meanings, ranging from fear to worship. Moreover, Bion's idea of the newborn as having a preconception of the breast may partly result from the stimulation of the oral area while sucking on the placenta, the thumb and the umbilical cord (Oster-weil 2002).

5 Etymologically, "caesura" comes from the Latin word meaning "cut" or "a cut-ting." In its literal sense, this term is used in surgery and also in poetry, where it relates to a pause/stop in the metrical rhythm of a verse. Generally speaking, both Freud and Bion use this term to designate differentiating states or events which seem to be completely separate from each other (for example, the prenatal and post-natal phases) but in reality are part of a continuous sequence, as is also true for gaps in a musical rhythm or in the beating of the heart.

6 See also Piontelli's warning in the postscript of her book (Piontelli 1992), highly relevant in the present context: "The facts of prenatal life, which previously had seemed to dominate and pervade all phantasies and games up to the age of four or five years, became intertwined and mixed with many additions and accretions belonging to later life. The composite picture one got at this later period, though still containing recognizable elements of their prenatal past, seemed fundamentally different from their previous straightforward and almost all-pervading linear ver-sion of their past. Prenatal life also seemed to lose its 'factual' realistic quality and became more and more colored and changed by the phantasy affect attached to it ... In the case of some children it became idealized; in the case of others it became charged with persecution and claustrophobic anxieties."

7 Bion's concept of O (1970) and Grotstein's emphasis on the ineffability of O (2000) expand the discussion on the search to understanding the mind and on the very limitations of this search.

8 The sense of an emergent self (from birth to the age of two months); the sense of a core, nuclear self (between two and six months); the sense of a subjective self (between seven and fifteen months) and the sense of a verbal self (after fifteen months) (Stern 1985). Thirteen years later, revisiting the original version of his book, Stern added two more layers in the hierarchy of the self: the "core self-with-another" preceding the subjective self, and the "narrative self" gradually developing out of the verbal self (Stern 1985), around the age of three or four, through early mother-child interactions that create "proto-narrative envelopes" (Stern 1995).

9 In his later writings, Mancia (2008) called this protostructure "the unrepressed unconscious."

References

Bianchedi, E.T.*et al.* (2002). Prenatals/postnatals: The total personality. In Alhanati, S. (ed.), *Primitive Mental States. Vol II: Psychological and Psychoanalytic Perspectives on Early Trauma and Personality Development*. New York: Karnac (a division of Other Press, LLC), 2002.

Bick, E. (1964). Notes on infant observation in psycho-analytic training. In Briggs, A. (ed.), *Surviving Space-Papers on Infant Observation*. London: Karnac, 2002.

Bion, W.R. (1962). *Learning From Experience*. London: Heinemann.

Bion, W.R. (1965). *Transformations*. London: Heinemann.

Bion, W.R. (1970). *Attention and Interpretation*. London: Tavistock.

Bion, W.R. (1975). *A Memoir of the Future, Book One: The Dream*. Rio de Janeiro: Imago.

Bion, W.R. (1977). *A Memoir of the Future, Book Two: The Past Presented*. Rio de Janeiro: Imago.

Bion, W.R. (1979). *A Memoir of the Future, Book Three: The Dawn of Oblivion*. Perthshire: Clunie.

Bowlby, J. (1980). *Attachment and Loss. Vol. III: Loss: Sadness and Depression*. New York: Basic Books.

Bowlby, J. (1988). *A Secure Base: Clinical Applications of Attachment Theory*. London: Routledge & Kegan Paul.

Briggs, A. (2002). *Surviving Space-Papers on Infant Observation*. London: Karnac.

Freud, S. (1914). *On Narcissism: An Introduction*. Standard Edition of the Complete Works of Sigmund Freud, 14: 67–104.

Gaddini, E. (1976). The invention of space in psychoanalysis. In *A Psychoanalytic Theory of Infantile Experience*. London: Routledge, 1992.

Gonzalez, F. (2010). Nothing comes from nothing: Failed births, dead babies. In van Buren, J. and Alhanati, S. (eds), *Primitive Mental States – A Psychoanalytic Exploration of the Origins of Meaning*. New York: Routledge, 2010.

Green, A. (1980). The dead mother. In Green, A., *On Private Madness*. Madison, CT: Int. Universities Press, 1986.

Grotstein, J. (1997). The psychoanalytic fascination with the concept of the "primitive". In Alhanati, S. and Kostoulas, K. (eds), *Primitive Mental States. Vol I: Across the Lifespan*. Northvale, NJ: Jason Aronson, 1997.

Grotstein, J. (2000). Bion's transformations in O. In *Who is the Dreamer Who Dreams the Dream? A Study of Psychic Presences*. New Jersey: The Analytic Press.

Grotstein, J. (2010). "Orphans of O": The negative therapeutic reaction and the longing for the childhood that never was. In van Buren, J. and Alhanati, S. (eds), *Primitive Mental States – A Psychoanalytic Exploration of the Origins of Meaning*. New York: Routledge, 2010.

Jung, C.G. (1936). *The Archetypes and the Collective Unconscious*. Tenth edition. New York: First Princeton/Bollingen Paperback, 1990.

Klein, M. (1928). Early stages of the Oedipus conflict. In *Contributions to Psycho-Analysis, 1921–1945*, pp. 202–214. London: Hogarth and the Institute of Psychoanalysis, 1950.

Klein, M. (1940). Mourning and its relation to manic-depressive states. In *Contributions to Psycho-Analysis, 1921–1945*, pp. 311–338. London: Hogarth and the Institute of Psychoanalysis, 1950.

Longfellow, H.W. (1883). *The Poetical Works of Henry Wadsworth Longfellow*. Boston: Houghton, Mifflin and Company.

Mahler, M. (1968). *On Human Symbiosis and the Vicissitudes of Individuation*. New York: International Universities Press.

Maiello, S. (1995). The sound object. *Journal of Child Psychotherapy*, 21(1): 23–42.

Mancia, M. (1981). On the beginning of mental life in the foetus. *International Journal of Psychoanalysis*, 62: 351–357.

Mancia, M. (1988). A note on Daniel Stern and the interpersonal world of the infant. *Rivista di Psicoanalisi*, 34: 176–192.

Mancia, M. (1989). On the birth of the self. *Rivista di Psicoanalisi*, 35: 1052–1072.

Mancia, M. (2008). The early unrepressed unconscious in relation to Matte-Blanco's thought. *International Forum of Psychoanalysis*, 17: 201–221.

Mitrani, J.L. (1996). Toward an understanding of unmentalized experience. In *A Framework for the Imaginary – Clinical Explorations in Primitive States of Being*. Northvale, NJ: Jason Aronson.

Mitrani, J.L. (1997). Further notes on an embryotic state of mind. In Alhanati, S. and Kostoulas, K. (eds), *Primitive Mental States. Vol I: Across the Lifespan*. Northvale, NJ: Jason Aronson, 1997.

Osterweil, E. (2002). Notes on the vicissitudes of intrauterine life. In Alhanati, S. (ed.), *Primitive Mental States. Vol II: Psychological and Psychoanalytic Perspectives on Early Trauma and Personality Development*. New York: Karnac (a division of Other Press, LLC), 2002.

Piontelli, A. (1986). *Backwards in Time: A Study in Infant Observation by the Method of Esther Bick*. Perthshire: Clunie.

Piontelli, A. (1992). *From Fetus to Child: An Observational and Psychoanalytic Study*. London: Routledge.

Piontelli, A. (2002). *Twins – From Fetus to Child*. London: Routledge.

Piontelli, A. (2010). *Development of Normal Fetal Movements: The First 25 Weeks of Gestation*. Milan: Springer-Verlag.

Ploye, P. (2006). *The Prenatal Theme in Psychotherapy*. London: Karnac.

Raskovsky, A. (1956). Beyond the oral stage. *International Journal of Psycho-Analysis*, 37: 286–289.

Rhode, E. (2003). *Notes on the Aniconic – The Foundations of Psychology in Ontology*. London: Apex One.

Rosenfeld, H. (1987). *Impasse and Interpretation: Therapeutic and Anti-Therapeutic Factors in Psychoanalytic Treatment of Psychotic, Borderline, and Neurotic Patients*. London: Tavistock.

Schellekes, A. (2009). *Discussion of Slochower, J. (2009): "Where's The Heat? When The Negative Transference Remains Elusive"*. Tel Aviv, Winnicott Center, June 2009.

Spitz, R. (1959). *A Genetic Field Theory of Ego Formation: Its Implications for Pathology*. New York: International Universities Press.

Stern, D. (1985). *The Interpersonal World of the Infant – A View from Psychoanalysis and Developmental Psychology*. New York: Basic Books, 1998.

Stern, D. (1995). *Motherhood Constellation: A Unified View of Parent-Infant Psychotherapy*. New York: Basic Books.

Stern, D. (2002). *The First Relationship – Infant and Mother*. Cambridge, MA: Harvard University Press.

Trevarthen, C. (1980). The foundations of intersubjectivity: Development of interpersonal and cooperative understanding in infants. In Olson, D. (ed.), *The Social Foundations of Language and Thought: Essays in Honor of J.S. Bruner*, pp. 316–342. New York: Norton.

Tustin, F. (1981). *Autistic States in Children*. London: Routledge & Kegan Paul.

Wilheim, J. (2010). The trauma of conception: Cellular memory. In van Buren, J. and Alhanati, S. (eds), *Primitive Mental States – A Psychoanalytic Exploration of the Origins of Meaning*. New York: Routledge, 2010.

Winnicott, D.W. (1949). Mind and its relation to psyche-soma. In *Through Paediatrics to Psychoanalysis*. London: Karnac, 1992.

Winnicott, D.W. (1960). The theory of the parent-infant relationship. In *The Maturational Processes and the Facilitating Environment: Studies in the Theory of Emotional Development*. The International Psycho-Analytical Library, 64, pp. 1–276. London: The Hogarth Press and the Institute of Psycho-Analysis.

Winnicott, D.W. (1962). Ego integration in child development. In *The Maturational Processes and The Facilitating Environment*. London: Hogarth Press, 1982.

Chapter 2

The dread of falling and dissolving[1]

In his book, *Love of Beginnings* (1993), Pontalis writes:

> ... I saw a man throw himself, smiling, from the top of the Eiffel Tower. He was wearing big wings. He had summoned journalists and cinematography. His fall was in a straight line. He crashed at the feet of officials in dark suits. I don't know his name. He was called the Bird Man. He had left no chance to chance as regards the preparations for his exploit.
>
> Several times a year, I see in my sleep aeroplanes of considerable size dive in free fall, as if naturally, into the small wood at the end of the garden at Boissy.
>
> We have invented words in order to escape from the law of gravity, in order to delay the fatal moment of the fall.

Titling that chapter of his book "The fall of bodies," Pontalis hints there at the difficulty and fear, characteristic of the human condition, of coming to terms with the dread of falling and death, and of finding words and meaning when faced with such a primary and overwhelming anxiety.

In this chapter, I would like to seek out words and meaning for the dread of falling and dissolving, two concepts thoroughly developed by Tustin (1986), a dread that inhabits some of our patients and some of us at certain moments. I would like to explore clinical material, theoretical thinking, literature and art that might enhance our understanding of these most primitive anxieties.

When I refer to falling, I do so, on the one hand, as a concrete event where the possibility of its happening arouses an anxiety that floods the psyche, and, on the other hand, as a metaphor standing for potential mental collapse, which is prone to occur when holding by a meaningful other is lacking and an internalization of a holding and containing presence has not yet crystallized. In the absence of such presence, the person feels scattered and unbounded, abandoned and in danger of falling out of the other's arms and forced to develop various defenses against the resulting flooding anxiety.

In order to befriend the subject, and to illustrate the movement between, at one pole, the dread of falling expressed as fear of the concrete event of falling

DOI: 10.4324/9781003479482-2

and, at the other pole, the fear of falling that appears in its more symbolic expressions, I would like to share with you some movements on this axis between the concrete and the symbolic in my own world.

The first stop on the axis is a childhood dream that recurred over the course of many years: in the dream, I was pedaling in the air, as if pushing the air downwards, and in this way steadily rising higher and higher above the ground. There was no direct expression in this dream or after it of a fear of falling, rather one of joy at the sensation of rising in the air. It seems to me that this joy expresses the reverse side, the negation of the dread of falling; that is to say, it expresses the experience of conquering gravity and of being, without danger of falling, high up in the air, far above the ground – the concrete and the human one. It is necessary, even if deducible, to point out that this dream of mine arose against a background of events that awoke an experience of powerlessness and falling away from the holding other. In other words, I want to emphasize how the metaphors in this dream expose the omnipotent and avoidant defense that enfolds and hides the fear of falling, in its intertwined physical and mental aspects.

The second stop on the axis between the concrete and the symbolic in the context of my present topic is an event from my adult life as a psychotherapist and psychoanalyst. In a first session with a patient who had come to therapy due to a difficult mental condition right before his marriage, we sat opposite each other. Danny, who was then 26 and had never had any intimate relations with a woman, suddenly found himself, in quite a passive way, in a relationship with his girlfriend that had proceeded by stages, as he experienced it, to a state preparatory to marriage. Danny's world was characterized by a fictitious efficiency and maturity. He was successful as a student, as a soldier and in his profession as an accountant, but apart from these successes, until meeting his wife-to-be, he lived in great emotional dependence on his parents, a kind of silent and dominated existence, as if without a voice and existence of his own, living frugally in emotional and social poverty. In this initial session, he recounted in an unbroken monotone, without facial expression, the evolution of his life. While listening to him, I told myself that Danny was in the throes of a panic attack, even though there was no concrete clinical sign of anxiety. I felt that this panic was that of a man forced all at once to leave a closed psychic retreat that he had built for himself, in a life experienced as an abyss that continually swallowed him. I listened intently for the whole hour, trying to discern what lay behind the story he was telling, verbose but devoid of emotion, and I particularly sensed the gap between the magnitude of his collapse and the abysmal paucity of his emotional life. As was a frequent habit of mine, I had been sitting cross-legged and, when the time approached to end the hour, I stood up to get the diary that was on my desk. Only after I had gotten up did I realize that one leg had completely gone to sleep without my having noticed it. As a result, by putting the load of my weight on this totally numb leg, it immediately buckled under, sending me sprawling on the floor of the consulting room in front of Danny. While all this was unfolding, Danny kept on recounting the story of his life without skipping a beat, in that constant monotone lacking any feeling, as if nothing had happened in front of his eyes. Full of pain, and after some moments of confusion and bewilderment, I told him that I had fallen … and that it was now necessary to end the session. We fixed a time for the next appointment, he got up and left, and I gathered myself from what turned out to be a bad sprain which immobilized me for a few days. In retrospect, I could see how on the stage of my body an intense drama had occurred, one that played out what in Danny's internal world was a tremendous drama, although not experienced emotionally by him and not represented: a part (of me) went to sleep completely and collapsed while another part went on functioning, and all this before the eyes of a blind other, who was emotionally dead, and who – it would seem – felt simultaneously abandoned and abandoning. In this event, there was no explicit sign of the dread of falling, only the fall itself, whose meaning as a reflection of ongoing emotional falling in Danny's life only became clear to me retroactively, part of it only years later.

The third and last axial point I will stop at is the period before preparing this chapter. Since that sprain, my left leg has retained a certain sensitivity, predisposing me to falls that I can usually control. But not so when, a few months before starting to work on this paper, I tripped in the street and fell badly. And so, that earlier sprain whose registration in my body accompanies me physically and emotionally expressed itself anew. Only after this second concrete fall did a deep fear of falling intensify in me, and a short dream sprang up some days later. In the dream, I was walking in the street with my son, who was two or three years old. The walk was along a steeply sloping road. Suddenly, he fell and rolled down the grassy slope, and I was afraid that he would be passive, do nothing and go on rolling down into the chasm. I shouted after him to resist the fall, to hold on to the grass and climb up until I could grasp his hand and pull him up. He began to struggle against the fall but held on to the grass and gave me his hand. The whole time I was terribly afraid that he might not reach my hand. However, inside the dream, I remembered that in reality he was actually an adolescent, so his oneiric face as a small child started alternating with that of the teenager. This prompted me, still within the dream, to tell myself that his fall was not possible, because he was a big boy. So much for the dream.

Of course, a lot of interpretations of this dream came to mind, but here I will highlight just one and leave the rest to your imagination and understanding. The emphasis I am choosing now is on the dream as reflecting a mental layer, which emerged following a concrete fall, and as describing a maternal failure starting with the fact that, while walking in the street, it was my son who was exposed to the precipice, ending with the fall itself. During the fall, the aspect that fell – be it one pertaining to my son or a regressed part of myself – whether in the past, present, or future (signified by the deadline of this paper) is overwhelmed by the dread of falling and sinks into the deep until there emerges a motherly voice that is actively enlisted – brings to life the falling part, gathers it up and stops the fall.

And now I would like to leave the personal plane and "fall into" theory. First, I want to recall and stress the importance in development of the acquisition of the ability to stand steadily and to move. Development of the self entails a firm connection to the sense of control and development of motor abilities, and the strengthening of these abilities allows every small child increasing independence and power. Winnicott's concept of "holding," which we use so frequently, describes in its concrete aspect the parents' physical holding of the baby, at a time when its level of maturity does not allow it to hold itself erect, and therefore the absence of parental holding would lead to the baby's fall. And further, during early development, on the basis of the external parental holding, an inner experience of the supporting object, a kind of mental spinal column (Anzieu 1989; Weissman 2009) becomes gradually solidified. This internal perception allows the integration of the experience of standing erect against gravitational force.

The developing motor independence also enables distance from the object, which at first happens on the physical plane, but soon physical distance turns into a movement that allows for mental life in the absence of the physical presence of the object. On a wider scale, we recognize the intense pleasure in childhood games involving running, jumping, skipping, climbing, flying through space. And in adulthood, we get these pleasures just the same, if in a more sophisticated way, expressed as pleasure through any physical activity where we conquer gravity, and have good control of our bodies' movements, without running the risk of falling. In this context, we can also think of the fascination we have for complicated circus acts and for any number of films with scenes where characters fly through the air while fighting each other, and for car chases where cars glide over obstacles that in reality no car would succeed in passing over (Katz 2002). Freud too, in *The Interpretation of Dreams* (1900), recalls the pleasure that a baby feels when it is thrown in the air and caught by an adult, a pleasure that is subsequently transformed into the wish to fly, by oneself, without the other's waiting arms being involved at all.

Analytic literature references to falling go through changes as a function of the development of analytic theories. So, in the same book (Freud 1900), Freud refers to falling in a dream as an expression of the seductiveness of sexual wishes, especially when he talks about women, who fall to/enjoy sexual seduction. In a more subtle way, in chapter 5 of *The Interpretation of Dreams*, a dream of Freud's appears where he tries to climb some stairs, joyously taking three at a time, until he meets a chambermaid coming down, and then suddenly he feels stuck to the stairs and unable to move. In this dream then, excitement connected with climbing becomes, according to Freud, an analogue for sexual excitement/arousal, along with its punishment, not quite expressed as falling but as paralysis of motor ability. Similar to Freud's paradigm, others (Freeman Sharpe 1951) also relate to falling as an expression of fear of impotence, guilt about sexual expression in general, and about masturbation in particular.

From another theoretical vertex, dreams are described where the dread of falling expresses the fear of loss of mental balance in different variants: loss of control, loss of consciousness, loss of conscience, and, in parallel, as an expression of the opposite wish – in other words, a wish to lose control and to free oneself altogether from demands and prohibitions (Saul & Curtis 1967; Gutheil 1951) and from an inner world that is choking and threatening. This reverse wish for omnipotent release sometimes appears in images that are the opposite of falling (as in my childhood dream) – that is, in images of gliding or flying. Fascinating in this regard is Winnicott's (1935) reference to the words "gravity," "grave," and "gravitation," words that are tied etymologically to matter, seriousness, weight and gravitational force pulling downwards, and in a symbolic way to the force of depression throwing us towards the depths. Winnicott well describes the manic defense which creates phantasies and experiences of omnipotent control over depressive feelings that flow from an unbearable inner reality. And so, the manic defense creates completely opposite situations: liveliness in place of death; movement in place of frozenness; lightness in place of heaviness, falling and depression. These sensations altogether make a person feel as if they have risen above the world.

The power to fly unaided is the highest victory over the force of gravity, apparently expressing a feeling of the greatest competence, but it is also possible to see in it an expression of the wish to return to the feeling of floating in the womb, where gravity has no impact, or in a more symbolic way, the wish to return to a uterine-like experience, without boundaries of time and space, thus denying the passage of time and ageing, a kind of wish to stay forever young, like Peter Pan, who flies freely (Wolf 1982).

Under the theoretical girder of ego psychology, and later on of theories of the self, the image of falling became an expression of conflict between archaic grandiose wishes and guilt about their existence, a guilt that leads to hostility towards the self, an experience of weakness and depletion of self-worth that is projected outwards in the image of falling (Saul & Curtis 1967; Gullestad 1994). So, for example, in folk stories from the countries of Eastern Europe, different versions (Antoniu 1996) appear of a craftsman who tries to build a glorious building, sometimes a gorgeous monastery, and everything he builds during the day crumbles and falls at night. Only when the builder sacrifices a close relative, usually a woman, and builds the building around her body while she is still alive – that is to say, pays the heaviest price for his extremely grandiose wishes – does the building acquire a secure foundation and cease to fall apart. The danger that lies in the primitive grandiose wish, before transformation and integration have come about, is well illustrated in the myth of Icarus, whose ability to fly so intoxicated him until, despite his father's warnings, he got too close to the sun and the wax that stuck his wings to his body melted, with the result that he fell into the sea and drowned. In a similar way, archaic grandiosity induced Tolstoy to jump at the age of nine from a high window, as if he believed he could transcend ordinary human ability and fly, an experience that ended in a serious fall and loss of consciousness for a day and a half, whereas Churchill, holding similar grandiose wishes, jumped at age 18 from a high place, again thinking that he could fly, an experience that ended in having a crushed body for months afterwards (Tolpin 1974). According to this theoretical understanding (Kohut 1966; Tolpin 1974), only when the first grandiosity is transformed and integrated into the other parts of the personality does it become an ability to fly not in a concrete sense but symbolically, intellectually, as the many successes surrounding Tolstoy and Churchill, at a later age, proved.

With the development of Tustin's writings (Tustin 1981, 1986, 1990) and of object relations theory in general (Klein 1946; Winnicott 1949, 1954a, 1954b, 1962; Bion 1970), the image of falling takes up more and more space and expresses an emotional, interpersonal matrix where the dominant feelings are those of a failure of holding, falling from the mother's womb or the analytic womb, or fear of disintegration of the self following such a fall. It seems to me that the image of falling not only expresses a deep anxiety but also enfolds within itself a complementary wish – that is, a desire to fall into a dependent and passive state, in the arms of the other, without control (Quinodoz 1997; Spoto 1976 in Berman 1997), as in expressions such as "falling asleep" or "falling in love" (Waugaman 1987).

Elsewhere (Schellekes 2005), I have described how the feeling of vertigo sometimes constitutes a sign of a fear of falling that is not just on the physical plane. Quinodoz (1997) describes various types of vertigo that are accompanied by an intense fear of falling and of losing one's physical or mental balance, each type of vertigo concealing a different constellation of object relations and each warning of the presence of the most primary anxieties. The most primitive type of vertigo that she describes is *fusion-related vertigo* (Quinodoz 1997, p. 21) – that is, vertigo that accompanies a condition of merging with the object. In this mental situation, the central anxiety is one of annihilation/dissolving of the self/loss-of-self anxiety. There is a complete undifferentiation between self and object, a sort of symbolic equation between the object and the self (Segal 1957), so that separation from, or annihilation of, the one is experienced as automatically causing the annihilation of the other, such that when the object gains distance the subject feels as if it fell inside itself, having leaked away and disappeared completely.

Before I expand theoretically on this situation, I would like to describe the case of Noah, a patient in his early twenties who sought therapy in a state of functional collapse, suicidal thoughts and acts of self-injury which eluded his awareness, and he had a severe sleep disorder. For many years, Noah had difficulty in falling asleep and slept for approximately three hours every night. When he approached me for therapy, Noah was staying at home doing nothing, crying for long hours and ceaselessly needing his mother, who used to sit for hours beside him stroking his forehead and wiping away his tears in a hopeless attempt to ease his awful distress. I met a man whose old appearance belied his young age, who moved with difficulty, as if every movement of slow and heavy walking was going to glue him to the ground. Likewise, his facial expression was frozen and changeless. It seemed to me that this heaviness and slowness enhanced an experience of stability and a kind of compensation for what I experienced as a lack of inner feeling of uprightness and inner grasp. Noah's life oscillated between lying in bed lethargically and spending long hours in a fitness club, where he achieved a very thin lower body and a thickened, muscular upper body, like the physique of a professional bodybuilder. Noah described his life as a series of placard-like events, as if he had passed through them without having lived, felt and remembered them; he spoke about his life as though reporting on another man's life, as if he were a sort of dead-alive person. He had fine intellectual talents, but he could not stand any situation that involved stress. Most of the time, he needed the immediate presence of the other, whose gaze was what determined his experience of himself but also held him in constant anxiety, because this gaze continued to be outside him, holding and haunting simultaneously; all this without his ability to actually sense himself, his thoughts, feelings, memories. In the sessions with me, his speech was slow and broken with long pauses as though lacking in tone and gradually fading away. Each question of mine would revive him for some moments, and he would adhere to what I had just said as if, with each question/remark, I had poured into him some stuffing essence that was viable only for a couple of minutes before he disappeared into a deathly silence – his gaze extinguished, as if any memory of vitality had dissolved. Apart from references to questions or other things I had said, there was no content that came from him, and the feeling of death in the room was choking. His existence was only matched to my movements as it was to his mother's or his friends' movements when they were right there beside him.

During this phase, I found myself creating a particular setting whereby, at the end of each session, we would schedule the next one or two meetings (even if these were almost invariably at the same time). I felt that the regular, pre-arranged and fixed time frame might be experienced by Noah as a kind of death, that the setting itself was liable to become a kind of autistic, mechanical object lacking any liveliness (Tustin 1986). I felt there was a need during every session to "inject" an interaction through which I was fighting to keep him alive, as when, at the end of each session, I consistently demanded his presence at the next meeting and thus became for him more of a "live company," "reclaiming" his presence, in Alvarez's terms (1992); and so I fought over the existence of each meeting and sometimes over every interaction during the sessions themselves. During these hours, I often felt that his silence was not a live silence, one that gives rise to feelings or thoughts, but rather a dead silence, where without my efforts to capture traces of feeling or thought in him, they would disappear completely in the abyss of oblivion. The sense of inner choking was so strong that it came as no surprise later to learn from Noah that he was asthmatic.

During our meetings, for long periods I felt that time stood still, that everything was frozen in place, that there was no movement, except when my eyelids closed as if from tiredness and a terrible heaviness, or whenever I shifted positions in the armchair; I experienced these micro-movements as something akin to needing oxygen when one is about to suffocate. I assume that some of my verbal interventions, in parallel to being intended for Noah and based on my understanding of him, also helped me feel that I was keeping myself alive, amidst the dissolution and evaporation we subsisted in. It soon became clear that in his childhood Noah could only fall asleep in the living room, surrounded by noise and human presence; and if he moved to his room, he would need the continuous presence, for hours, of one of his parents if he was to fall asleep for a little while. He recounted that when, as a child, he had asked, "What is death?" he was told that death was like sleep, except one from which we do not wake up. It was his way of communicating how sleep, since it implies giving up control, became a situation whereby he felt as if he were dissolving into himself, and how wakefulness constituted a perpetual battle for his life, a mighty effort against leaking away.

Over a long period, the sessions were characterized by long silences, where the central event was my attempt to move the hands of the clock with my thoughts, without any success. The feeling was not of something empty but of a terrible frozenness. We sat for hours in this silence, without any content. Sometimes I would ask a short question such as "Where are you?," and then Noah would answer, "I don't know. I am straining to find a thought, any thought," and during this straining I felt that his blood vessels were ready to burst from the strain, and that simultaneously my breathing had become slow and heavy. An attempt to allow a measure of relief from this strain pressured him terribly because, as I gradually began to understand, the experience of straining constituted a mental muscle, a holding, a living event that was needed as a means of survival during those moments. After a number of months, Noah began to speak, each time a little more, and the sessions turned into a sequence of silence and speech, being and disappearing, a sequence that in my experience allowed the existence of tolerable intervals, whereby a process of fragmentary thinking began to form. Noah revived when he spoke, as if by speaking to me he could feel alive – as if every time I found any interest or meaning in his words it imparted to him a meaning that did not exist before. Mostly he told me, step by step, how he was doing more, how he dared to be active in ways he had not dared before, and gradually his functioning, at least his professional studies, went very well, despite the terrible anxiety that had beset him initially.

When his psyche began to move a little more, he recounted the following dream:

> I am sleeping on a bed, on one of New York's crowded avenues, surrounded by masses of people and buildings. Opposite my bed is a clothes stall, where occasionally I try to put on a shirt, but each shirt I try is stained.

I will not detail all the work done around the dream but will only emphasize how, despite the immediate feeling I had that the imagery of the dream – a homeless person without adequate clothing – depicted a scene of distress and lack of a protective sheath, Noah described the feeling in the dream as one of happiness. He emphasized how he felt serene and happy amidst the noise and tumult, as if millions of people and buildings wrapped him up, and only this way could he sleep (like in the tumult of the living room at home).

It seems to me that in this state, fusion with the environment, as appears in Noah's dream, is an attempt to block the experience of a black hole (Tustin 1986) that threatens to draw him into nullity and annihilation. Adhesion to, and fusion with, the object creates an illusion that the object is part of the self, and this acts as a defensive activity against the terror of separateness, which is equivalent to an experience of mental death. When he was alone, in the absence of any external holding, and in the absence of an internal, holding and organizing mental spinal column, Noah stayed awake, alert, tense, and this alertness, similarly to the muscles he developed, created a feeling of hardness like a second skin (Bick 1968). This skin built an illusion of blocked holes through which he was otherwise in danger of evaporating. These holes do not have a mental representation, but they disseminate the essence of their presence as holes as if they were particles of dust that spread into every level of the mental experience, creating behaviors or feelings that precisely reflect the potential for disappearing into the hole.

This world of intense fused relations is characterized by a lack of three dimensionality and of an internal space needed to process psychic experiences. This is a two-dimensional world in which the main defense is adhesive identification, as described by Bick (1986), Gaddini (1969), Meltzer et al. (1975), Tustin (1986), and Mitrani (1994). Adhesive identification is the result of a failure to internalize the containing function of the parent; this failure causes an inability to grasp the self and the object as having an internal space and qualities typical of a whole object. Actually, in this situation, we are not talking of identification in the classical sense, but rather of imitation of the most superficial aspects of the object and of adhesion to the object, as an illusion of being held that prevents the experience of falling and fragmentation.

In this description of Noah, I have chosen to emphasize how his psychic existence was like a leaking self, as if he were made of a hollowed ego skin/envelope, to use Anzieu's language (1989) (see also Keinan 2009). Noah lived in an environment where his parents' anxiety, especially death anxiety and in particular that of his mother, was extremely high and created a continuous heavy physical presence of his mother, one that flooded his whole existence with anxiety. Even today his parents come to check in on his sleep a number of times a night. Since at every moment he is liable to disappear, at every moment they must be present. This way the physical, uninterrupted presence became a mental absence. Instead of a representation of a regulating and calming first skin (Bick 1968; Anzieu 1989) that acts as an enveloping sheath, holding the psyche at the beginning of its development, a perforated sheath was created, leaving Noah sucked in and flooded by anxiety. According to Eigen, an inundating human presence creates a short circuit in a soul that is not well enough equipped, and this short circuit translates into annihilation of thought, feeling and vital energy. In his words, "The blankness of too much is replaced by the blankness of nothing" (Eigen 1996, p. 8).

In this condition, the sense of stuck-ness and of being sucked up by a void is prominent, as reflected in expressions such as "quicksand" and "black hole." It was Tustin (1981, 1986, 1990) and, following her, Grotstein (1990), Mitrani (1992, 1994), Eigen (1996), Eshel (1998), and Schellekes (2019) who described the experience of falling into a black hole, into a void, out of existence. All these expressions describe a flimsy constellation of object relations where the self feels completely unheld; and in the absence of any contact with a human object, even of an adhesive type, the person's ability to survive psychically collapses, and an experience of falling into the abyss occurs.

We are not talking here about an emptiness that derives from the primary anxiety which is activated by the death drive creating terror of destruction and annihilation, as Klein (1946) well describes, but about a primary state of deficit and lack of a holding structure, a void mental structure (see also Schellekes 2013, 2019). In this state, the dominant anxiety is more one of dissolving and losing one's sense of existence than one of a defense like dissociation or splitting because these latter defenses express strong feelings related to a matrix of object relations, while in the void structure a lack of object representations prevails.

Using Noah's case, I emphasized how a flooding presence may turn into a death-provoking one, since such a presence creates an emotional excess that obstructs object internalization. What I mean to stress is how, in this condition, no differentiation exists between the object and the subject, differentiation which is essential to the development of a mental space. This development closely depends on internalizing the containing object, an internalization that constitutes the primary representation of the experience of three-dimensionality and of an inner space for processing experiences (Bick 1968, 1986; Meltzer et al. 1975; Grotstein 1978). In other words, I am emphasizing here how meaningful the absence of the object is, as long as it is in a dosage that can be digested, since during such absences buds of thought begin to emerge, as described by many writers such as Freud, Bion, Winnicott and Green (Freud 1917; Bion 1959; Winnicott 1949, 1951, 1953; Green 1983).

Stating things differently, the internalized presence makes it possible to imagine the object in its absence, through different hallucinatory activities, as if the object were present. The absence gives rise in this context to vitality, creativity and thought, thanks to the introjected construction of a framing structure (Green 1999) that holds the mind in a similar way to how a mother's arms hold the baby's body. This structure ensures that the *non-presence* of the object will not turn into the *non-existence* of the subject. When the absence is too traumatic or goes on for longer than one can bear, it does not generate creativity and thought but loss of meaning and inner death, as Green (1983) aptly describes when he talks about the absent presence of the dead mother that creates states of emptiness, void, non-existence, meaninglessness and frozenness. The experience of a negative presence builds, as Green puts it well, "an inner representation of the absence of representation" (Green 1999, p. 208) – that negative hallucination which becomes life's central pivot and leads to loss of memory, loss of a sense of self, loss of vitality and contact, and inability to experience human contact even when it is potentially available. In this connection, I recall the Israeli film *Lovesick on Nana Street*, [2] where the central character cries longingly throughout the film for Evelyn, his beloved, and in a moving scene near the end, when Evelyn is beside him, he goes on painfully calling out her name, without seeing her, as if she were not there, right next to him.

In a fascinating way, Gaddini (1976, 1980) continues Winnicott's thinking (Winnicott 1974) about the fear of falling apart/of breakdown and describes his understanding of loss-of-self anxiety. According to Gaddini, in normal development, the initial formation of a separate sense of self is bound up with an experience of a catastrophic split that occurred when the sense of a total and omnipotent self disappeared. Traces of this split persist in the mind forever, and every developmental move towards a sense of premature separateness is immediately absorbed and echoes the initial rending. The more traumatic and painful this initial rupture and experiences of separation were, the more intensified the loss-of-self anxiety becomes, echoing the catastrophic experience that already happened at the beginning of development, when the sense of the total self was lost. According to Gaddini, loss-of-self anxiety constitutes a defense, a kind of watchfulness, so that the initial catastrophic experience will not be re-experienced. The deeper the loss-of-self anxiety, the more the mind enlists every means at its disposal to get back omnipotent control. And so Noah stands on guard, clinging to parental figures, not sleeping, taut like a spring, walking slowly so that every step glues him heavily to the ground, gathering every bit of himself into his muscles, hardly being able to think, feel, remember.

In these adhesive pseudo-object relations (Mitrani 1994) that are so evident in Noah's life, the central mode of experience is through imitation, as if by imitation the presence of the lost and not yet internalized object is reconstructed (Gaddini 1969; Green 1983). The symptomatic mental state that often develops in this situation, whether in a psychosomatic symptom (Gaddini 1980) or in an experience of inner death, illustrates the existence of an intrusive object, an "interject" in the language of Bollas (1999), whose penetrating presence breaks the natural sequential process of development and creates a sense of blocking, hesitancy, emptiness, muteness and mental death.

If we return to Quinodoz's view of different types of vertigo that enfold a variety of fears of falling, the fusion-related vertigo emphasizes, as previously mentioned, a mental state wherein the psychic existence of one is totally dependent on the existence of the other, and the disappearance of the one leads to annihilation of the other/loss-of-self anxiety. In contrast to this type of vertigo, Quinodoz describes a feeling of dizziness to do with fear of losing connection with the object, which she calls "vertigo related to being dropped" (Quinodoz 1997, p. 33). This is anxiety about loss of the object's love. The fear is of loss of continuous contact and connection with the object, while the object is experienced as rejecting, disappointing, frustrating, abandoning, aborting. However, we are not talking about falling that leads to annihilation and fragmentation of the self but about falling from the arms of the containing other while the self remains whole. Here the object does not collapse together with the self; the two are not fused but differentiated, even if this differentiation is felt as very painful. Neither the self nor the object is annihilated, and there is no danger of mutual collapse. Certainly, in this situation one feels haunted and threatened, but one does not become extinguished or broken up. Actually, the anxiety connected to fusion with the object is not put in terms of fear of falling but of anxiety about fading away, fainting, and losing oneself, of losing one's memory and sense of continuity, a feeling of extreme estrangement, inner death, being emptied out and dissolved, going as far as loss of psychic existence. In contrast, the fear of falling from the hands of the object and losing its love assumes that the self is sufficiently crystallized and continues to exist while it is falling and thereafter, as Tustin rightly emphasizes when she differentiates between falling and being spilled or dissolved (Tustin 1986). In other words, fear of falling from the other's hands takes place when some ability to contain has been internalized, when an inner representation of the object exists, functioning as a kind of mental spine which holds and demarcates one's existence and prevents the total falling that leads to the annihilation of the self.

A similar thinking to Quinodoz's concept of fear of falling from the hands of the holding other (vertigo related to being dropped) is found in Ferenczi's writings many years earlier, in a short article (Ferenczi 1914) where he describes situations at the end of an analytic hour where the analysand feels a sort of vertigo (giddiness) on getting up from the couch. Ferenczi interpreted this phenomenon as a bodily sensation arising at the transition, in time and space, between one's conduct following the pleasure principle and conduct following the reality principle – in Freudian terms – and as expressing a feeling of being torn apart from the analytic holding – in the language of object relations. Similar to this, Winnicott (1949, 1954a, 1954b) relates to falling from the couch as an analogue of the experience of falling from the analytic lap, which is itself a re-experience of birth and separation trauma, with a concomitant wish to be scooped up by the analyst from the depths of falling, not unlike the wish expressed in my dream about my son's fall. In other words, the feeling of dizziness at the end of an analytic session, coupled with fear of falling, may function as a signal coming from the patient's body and warning of the analyst's containment failure. And retrospectively, we can see in my dream, in which my son fell into the deep, a close connection to Noah's treatment, a kind of signal warning me of the experience of holding failure during his therapy.

I would like to illustrate now the dialectic between loss-of-self anxiety, in its different varieties, and fear of falling, by contemplating some works of art. First, I will focus on Francis Bacon's masterful depictions of human figures who are distorted, damaged and hollow and who have lost their contents, lacking definition and boundary. In this way, Bacon shows the loss-of-self anxiety on the stage of a body that is deformed and losing its humanity (van Alphen 1992). For example, in the series of paintings called *Triptych May-June 1973*, a man is portrayed in three different situations.[3] To the left and right of the triptych, a man appears to be secreting into a toilet bowl and basin, respectively – his body crumpled and drawn downward. In the middle image, we are witnesses to the peak moment of this emptying out, when the man is poured into his own shadow, when all the contents of his body disappear into the shadow/the black hole, leading to the loss of human form and identity. The shadow does not confirm identity, as is often shown in art (Schellekes 2006, 2010), but stands for loss of identity and the emptying out of the self. The difficult drama represented in these pictures is reproduced in the viewer, who, through his or her senses, feels acute distress and unease in their own body. Perhaps as a defense, many of Bacon's characters are located in separate, protective frames, as is the case in the picture *Three Studies of Lucian Freud* (1969),[4] but we can quickly see how this defense is actually a sort of imprisonment, since every character is isolated, and the frame not only fails to protect but also cleaves the subject, again at the level of the body, of the senses. In Bacon's paintings, the deformation is nearly always of the head, the main site of the senses, and in particular we see it in the split of sight, which partly turns towards the self and partly towards the viewer, partly expressing the state of being observed and partly that of observing (van Alphen 1992). One way or another, most of the characters do not have any human contact, and hints of a possible contact only emphasize its impossibility. Means such as lights, mirrors and cameras which are expected to return or reflect the self back to itself fail to do so and instead bring the self back to its experience of itself as dissolved or split. So, for example, in *Portrait of George Dyer in a Mirror* (1967–1968),[5] the reflection in the mirror is not of the figure facing the mirror but of the view of the spectator of the picture who sees the missing part of the represented figure. Here we are again witnessing a cleaving split, without it being clear whether the split and the deformation are in the mirror, in the view of the character of himself or between the gaze of the spectator and the gaze of the character. Certainly, the large number of mirrors in Bacon's works hints at the object's non-existence and at an exaggerated use of the narcissistic defense, which leads to heightened awareness and watchfulness of the self in an attempt to prevent the self from falling apart.

I have chosen to illustrate another way of showing the fear of dissolving and fading away through some works of Dali's, who was tormented by his preoccupation with the dimension of time, loss of the sense of time and loss of memory. In his famous painting, *The Persistence of Memory* (1931),[6] we are aware of Dali's struggle to depict time as fluid and soft just as his soft clocks show. He was preoccupied with the constancy and continuity of memory, particularly against the background of a lack of liveliness and humanity, as is amply illustrated by the images in the painting (a lifeless landscape, a desert, a dead bird, and so on). In another, less known, painting of his, *The Disintegration of The Persistence of Memory* (1952–1954),[7] we see a version of the earlier picture, but this time during fragmentation and disintegration. Highlighted in parallel with the experience of fragmentation is the effort to find control over it, which in the painting appears, in my opinion, as precise squares separated by identical and exact spaces between disintegrated and fragmented objects, all flooded by water.

In contrast to the preoccupation with the dissolution of the self, Magritte presents a series of paintings where the recurrent theme is falling but without the object losing its identity or wholeness, in accordance with the distinction I tried to make between fear of dissolving of the self and fear of falling. So, in the painting *Golconda* (1953),[8] multiple Magritte doubles appear that might be falling or might be floating in the air, the latter negating the force of gravity. In his 1959 painting *The Castle in the Pyrénées*,[9] we see an extremely hard rock/castle whose very solidity makes one wonder if it is floating in the air or falling. Here as well, effort is put into emphasizing the unbreakable solidity of the castle opposite to and against a background of the fluid qualities of the sea and the airiness of the sky. At least on the visual level the castle is highlighted as whole and strong, even if in danger of a serious fall that, should it happen, we can suppose will not lead to the shattering of the castle but of everything else beneath it. Perhaps it is worthwhile to remember here that Magritte lost his mother at age 13 to suicide by drowning in the river beside their home, and that according to his report he also saw her body being pulled from the river. Loss of contact with the object or, in the language of Quinodoz (1997), fear of falling from the object, continues as a central subject in the work of Magritte, where past trauma is present in nearly every work, whether directly or through refuting the existence of trauma.

Inspired by Magritte's *The Castle in the Pyrénées*, the contemporary Polish artist Jacek Yerka painted *Cowan City* (1993).[10] In this painting, a kind of multi-layered and heavily weighted structure appears to have merged with a tree abundant in roots. At first glance, we are led to sense that the stability of the structure is self-evident, obviating any imminent danger of falling, but on a second look we can see that the whole structure is actually not connected to stable ground at all; rather, it floats above the clouds, and so all the means through which we came to experience the firmness of the structure take on an additional, deceptive aspect because they cannot remove the danger of a potential fall.

Both the dread of being rejected or dropped by the object (and consequently of losing contact with the object) and the dread of annihilation appear in dramatic ways in Beckett's short story *The Expelled* (1946), which was written while Beckett was living in France. It is probably the second story written by him in French, after he had expelled himself from his motherland, Ireland, and from his mother tongue, English. The story begins with the narrator's memory of the pain involved in the obsessive counting he used to engage in as a child. He used to count the steps of his house and get mixed up in the process, never being able to decide whether he should include the sidewalk as the first step or not. As an adult, the storyteller makes a great effort to remember the number of steps, alas to no avail. As for remembering, Beckett (1946, pp. 46–47) proclaims:

> Memories are killing. So you must not think of certain things, of those that are dear to you, or rather you must think of them, for if you don't there is the danger of finding them, in your mind, little by little. That is to say, you must think of them for a while, a good while, every day several times a day, until they sink forever in the mud. That's an order.

This text illustrates, in my opinion, in the tragic–comic way typical of Beckett, the effort to control the black shadow of the object upon one's soul. According to Beckett, the more the child is absorbed in obsessive counting, the less he will think of the persons who inflict unbearable pain and anxiety on him, or at the very least he will have the illusion that he controls their impact on him.

Later in the story, we begin to understand against what such heavy defenses are needed. The child in the story had been thrown out of his house into the street. Although the concrete number of steps might have been relatively small and the physical fall from them might not have been too painful, it is quite easy to imagine the intensity of the emotional fall when a child is being thrown out of his house by his parents. The immediate comfort the child found was the sound of the door slam that followed his being thrown out. This sound made it clear for him that his parents did not intend to pursue him down the street with a stick, to beat him in full view of the passersby, but "just" to expel him into the street. The second consolation was built up in the child's mind by registering the fact that he had been thrown out into the street with his hat on, which had been his duty to wear at all times, so as not to trigger his father's envy of the son's handsome and young head. So, this hat, though it had been bought under duress and though it made kids mock him, became for the narrator an item never to part from, not even after his father's death. The hat became inseparable from him, demarcating and defining him. When he is thrown out and falls into the street, the child knows that he has lost the only home he ever had. When he has a final look back at the house from which he has been expelled, he sees his family cleaning his room and spraying it with disinfectant. He starts walking, and here, not incidentally, Beckett describes in great detail the grammar of his walk and of his "nether rigidity" (Beckett 1946, p. 51) – the stiffening of his lower limbs and the splaying of his feet wide apart, to the right and left of the line of march, while desperately rolling his bust. In spite of the extreme effort invested so as to control every step and achieve a stable position, his trunk is felt to be "flabby as an old ragbag" (Beckett 1946, p. 50), his walk is shaky and he often loses his balance and falls. He remembers how, as a child, he used to keep his feces in his pants for hours, refusing to change or be helped by his mother.

According to this description, it seems that the burn felt on the skin of his bottom and the stink became for this child a vital means of holding and maintaining his self, comparable to the function of smell as a protecting psychic envelope, as described by Anzieu (1989) and Ogden (1989).

Similarly, it seems that the narrator's walking in an extremely controlled and rigid bodily posture strives to balance his shaken mental and physical equilibrium. We witness not infrequently the formation of a secondary skin (Bick 1968), which is evident when an extreme mental or physical muscularity is defensively developed to contain one's soul, when the parental containing function has not been internalized and a mental column/structure, as previously described, has not been established. Beckett accurately details how the narrator developed his obsession to control his body through rigid maneuvers so as to hide his internal weakness and the stink of his feces, both being signs of mental leakage through his hollowed-out body and mind. After the expulsion into the street, the narrator starts walking with his legs spread wide apart so that no one can walk beside him on the sidewalk. He almost runs over a child, which would have pleased him, since he detests children. In Beckett's language, "I personally would lynch them with the utmost pleasure, I don't say I'd lend a hand, no, I am not a violent man, but I'd encourage the others and stand them drinks when it was done" (Beckett 1946, p. 52). In his biting words, Beckett describes the narrator's hate that conceals his envy towards children who are, in his opinion, undeservedly granted so much happiness and tolerance. Although the narrator does not kill anyone, walking along the street he falls and brings down with him an old lady (probably a displaced image of his mother), hoping her bones will thus be broken. He is reprimanded by a policeman, who says that he should leave room for others while walking on the sidewalk, or otherwise he had better stay at home. Beckett adds in his typical cynicism: "And that he should attribute to me a home was no small satisfaction" (Beckett 1946, p. 52). Later on, he gets into a cab, searches his memory for an address so as to justify his travel, thinks of buying the cab without the horse, and hires it for one day. Thus it seems that the cab is experienced by him as a sort of protecting space reminiscent of something between a cradle and a home. He invites the cab driver to have lunch with him, to help him find a room to let; they talk about their lives and do their best to understand, to explain. The warm contact that develops between the cabman and the expelled character is especially moving since, in the background, we still breathe the heavy abandonment that fills every corner of the narrator's world. In Beckett's words, "He had preferred me to a funeral, this was a fact which would endure forever" (Beckett 1946, p. 57). As he is enveloped by the cab and by this thin layer of human contact, momentarily some warmth and even a capacity to care fill the expelled man's heart. He registers the cabman's worries, offers to help him light the cab lamps, and feels concern for the overworked and tired horse. At the end of the day, he is invited to sleep in the driver's home and agrees to do so only if he can sleep in the stables. While there, he hears the voices of the cabman and his wife and imagines that they are criticizing him. He gets into the carriage and has the urge to set it on fire but does not do so; instead, he gets out and leaves some money as a sign of gratitude before regretting this act, retrieving the money, and expelling himself back into the street.

Throughout all his writings, Beckett vividly describes the despair and hopelessness that underlie a lack of human contact and the frustrated, yet never-ending, yearning for human contact. The theme of falling that appears so often in his writings represents, in my view, the primary catastrophic fall, the break in child–parent relations. Against this rupture (Keller 2002), Beckett describes various psychic retreats (Steiner 1993), internal refuges from human contact, internal places for rest and eventual restoration of hunger for human contact. The schizoid retreat with obvious contiguous-autistic (Ogden 1989) features becomes the only option available, since human contact is perceived as causing the loss of one's self. As Beckett expresses it, "We are alone. We cannot know and cannot be known. Man is the creature that cannot come forth from himself, who knows other only in himself, and who, if he asserts the contrary, lies" (Beckett in Keller 2002, p. 178).

In *The Expelled*, the expelling and falling become simple images symbolizing psychological abortion. The narrator can rest neither in his home nor in his body, nor in the human environment in which he lives. The throwing out of the child is a vivid image of being dropped out of the mother's soul and of becoming physically and mentally homeless. It seems that we find here an expression of what Quinodoz called the fear of being dropped, a situation where the storyteller is not annihilated and remains whole. However, one can find many hints in the story that this being dropped from the parental container follows extreme early experiences in which the danger of self-dissolution is expressed mainly through the defenses built against this fear, such as the habit of keeping his excrement as a warming/burning blanket around his body. So it appears that the later fall becomes mingled with a much earlier one in which dissolution and the leaking of the self took place. Against both the dread of dissolution and the dread of losing contact with the object, the narrator finds his only solution: Retreat from human contact and refuge in the body, which somehow becomes his only shelter. No wonder he refuses to part from his feces; no wonder he develops such a stiff and rigid way of walking, which aims at holding him as if he were made of concrete; no wonder he lives in hate and seclusion. The yearning for human contact does not disappear, and for seconds he feels connected to the cabman. But soon he cannot stand the pain and humiliation of being in need of contact. He rapidly feels criticized by the driver, and this time he expels (drops) himself into the street and into loneliness, into his internal world filled with persecuting object representations.

The main experience aroused by this story and others by Beckett is of a human being imprisoned in a closed space that is aimed to protect, but in which one cannot move and cannot breathe (Meltzer 1992). Moving away from this space is dangerous to the self that feels haunted by its early objects to such an extent that inertness and feeling at a standstill become the main affective venues. Yet there is no total forswearing of human contact, and one keeps oscillating between yearning for contact and fearing its threatening, paralyzing power.

One can say that, in Beckett's story, we encounter a gloomy world wherein most of the motion is downward, toward collapse, toward survival through schizoid retreat into loneliness, hate, and disconnection. However, I suggest we remember that although Beckett himself had been deeply marked and haunted by especially severe experiences in his early childhood he was successful in creating tremendously rich and fascinating writings. One can assume that the act of writing became the very container of the hard contents he wrote about. Moreover, his self-imposed expulsion from his mother tongue was followed, much later in his life, by his linguistic "home-coming," in that he translated his writings, mostly unaided, back into English.

I have attempted in this chapter to start from Tustin's description of the most primitive anxieties, those of falling and dissolving, and to play around with her concepts in a way that can expand our clinical and theoretical understanding. I daresay that my own preoccupation with this subject is an attempt to inch forward on the continuum where, at one pole, in our most frightening moments, we are in danger of falling into the realm of bodily, concrete, wordless, and sometimes meaningless experiences. At the other pole, however, we may succeed in using the most dreadful experiences as an incentive for internal reorganization and change – in other words, as a means of overcoming those ruptures that lurk in the corners of the soul.

Notes

1 This paper received the 12th Frances Tustin Memorial Prize in 2008 and was presented in November 2008 at the Annual International Frances Tustin Memorial Lectureship Day in Los Angeles, at the Psychoanalytic Center of California (PCC). It was published in 2019 and is reproduced here with the permission granted by the *British Journal of Psychotherapy*: Schellekes, A. (2019). The dread of falling and dissolving – Further thoughts. *British Journal of Psychotherapy, 35(3)*: 448–467.
2 *Lovesick on Nana Street* is a 1995 Israeli movie, directed by Shabi Gabinzon.
3 This work can be seen at the website of The Francis Bacon Estate: https://francis-bacon.com/life/family-friends-sitters/george-dyer/triptych-may-june
4 This work can be seen at: https://www.francis-bacon.com/artworks/paintings/three-studies-lucian-freud
5 This work can be seen at: https://www.francis-bacon.com/artworks/paintings/portrait-george-dyer-mirror
6 This work can be seen at the Salvador Dali Paintings website: https://www.dalipaintings.com/persistence-of-memory.jsp
7 This work can be seen at: https://www.dalipaintings.com/the-disintegration-of-the-persistence-of-memory.jsp
8 This work can be seen at renemagritte.org: https://www.renemagritte.org/golconda.jsp
9 This work can be seen at: https://www.renemagritte.org/the-castle-of-the-pyrenees.jsp
10 This work can be seen at the website Yerkaland: https://www.yerkaland.com/?attachment_id=1228

References

Alvarez, A. (1992). *Live Company: Psychotherapy with Autistic, Borderline, Deprived and Abused Children*. London: Routledge.

Antoniu, M. (1996). The walled-up bride: An architecture of eternal return. In Coleman, D.L., Danze, E.A. and Henderson, C.J. (eds), *Architecture and Feminism*. New York: Princeton Architectural Press, 1996.

Anzieu, D. (1989). *The Skin Ego*. New Haven, CT: Yale University Press, French edition, 1985.

Beckett, S. (1946). The Expelled. In Gontarski, S.E. (ed.), *Samuel Beckett: The Complete Short Prose*, pp. 46–61. New York: Grove Press, 1995.

Berman, E. (1997). Hitchcock's vertigo: The collapse of a rescue fantasy. *International Journal of Psychoanalysis*, 78: 975–988.

Bick, E. (1968). The experience of the skin in early object relations. *International Journal of Psychoanalysis*, 49: 484–486.

Bick, E. (1986). Further considerations on the function of the skin in early object relations. *British Journal of Psychotherapy*, 2(4): 292–301.

Bion, W.R. (1959). Attacks on linking. *International Journal of Psychoanalysis*, 40: 308–315.

Bion, W.R. (1970). *Attention and Interpretation*. London: Tavistock.

Bollas, C. (1999). Dead mother, dead child. In Kohon, G. (ed.), *The Dead Mother – The Work of Andre Green*. London: Routledge, 1995.

Eigen, M. (1996). *Psychic Deadness*. Northvale, NJ and London: Jason Aronson.

Eshel, O. (1998). 'Black holes', deadness and existing analytically. *International Journal of Psychoanalysis*, 79: 1115–1130.

Ferenczi, S. (1914). Sensations of giddiness at the end of the psycho-analytic session. In *Further Contributions to the Theory and Technique of Psycho-Analysis*, pp. 239–241. London: Hogarth, 1926.

Freeman Sharpe, E. (1951). *Dream Analysis*. London: Hogarth Press.

Freud, S. (1900). *The Interpretation of Dreams*. Standard Edition of the Complete Works of Sigmund Freud, 4–5.

Freud, S. (1917). *Mourning and Melancholia*. Standard Edition of the Complete Works of Sigmund Freud, 14: 237–258.

Gaddini, E. (1969). On imitation. *International Journal of Psychoanalysis*, 50: 475–484.

Gaddini, E. (1976). The invention of space in psychoanalysis. In *A Psychoanalytic Theory of Infantile Experience*. London: Routledge, 1992.

Gaddini, E. (1980). Notes on the mind-body question. In *A Psychoanalytic Theory of Infantile Experience*. London: Routledge, 1992.

Green, A. (1983). The dead mother. In *On Private Madness*. London: Hogarth Press, 1986.

Green, A. (1999). The intuition of the negative in 'Playing and Reality'. In Kohon, G. (ed.), *The Dead Mother – The Work of Andre Green*. London: Routledge, 1999.

Grotstein, J.S. (1978). Inner space: Its dimensions and its coordinates. *International Journal of Psychoanalysis*, 59: 55–61.

Grotstein, J.S. (1990). Nothingness, meaninglessness, chaos and the "black hole": I. The importance of nothingness, meaninglessness and chaos in psychoanalysis. *Contemporary Psychoanalysis*, 26: 257–290.

Gullestad, S.E. (1994). Fear of falling – Some unconscious factors in Ibsen's play "The Master Builder". *The Scandinavian Psychoanalysis Review*, 17: 27–39.

Gutheil, R.M. (1951). *The Handbook of Dream Analysis*. New York: Liveright.

Katz, H.M. (2002). Escaping gravity. *The Psychoanalytic Study of the Child*, 57: 294–304.

Keinan, N. (2009). The hollowed envelope – On the therapeutic work with "holes" in the psyche. *Sihot-Dialogue, Israel Journal of Psychotherapy*, 23(2).

Keller, J.R. (2002). *Samuel Beckett and the Primacy of Love*. Manchester: Manchester University Press.

Klein, M. (1946). Notes on some schizoid mechanisms. *International Journal of Psychoanalysis*, 27: 99–110.

Kohut, H. (1966). Forms and transformations of narcissism. *Journal of the American Psychoanalytic Association.*, 14: 243–272.

Meltzer, D.*et al.* (1975). *Explorations in Autism*. Perthshire: Clunie.

Meltzer, D. (1992). *The Claustrum – An Investigation of Claustrophobic Phenomena*. Perthshire: Clunie.

Mitrani, J. (1992). On the survival function of autistic maneuvers in adult patients. *International Journal of Psychoanalysis*, 73(2): 549–560.

Mitrani, J. (1994). On adhesive-pseudo-object relations: Part I – Theory. *Contemporary Psychoanalysis*, 30(2): 348–366.

Ogden, T. (1989). The autistic-contiguous position. In *The Primitive Edge of Experience*. Northvale, NJ: Jason Aronson, 1989.

Pontalis, J-B. (1993). *Love of Beginnings*. London: Free Association.

Quinodoz, D. (1997). *Emotional Vertigo – Between Anxiety and Pleasure*. New Library of Psychoanalysis. London: Routledge.

Schellekes, A. (2005). The dread of falling: Between breaking one's back and breaking through. *Psychoanalytic Dialogues*, 15(6): 897–908.

Schellekes, A. (2006). *Shadow and Double: Illusions of Identity, Presence and Absence.* Lecture given at the joint conference "Double-Double" of The Program of Psycho-analytic Psychotherapy, Faculty of Medicine and The Faculty of Philosophy, Tel-Aviv University.

Schellekes, A. (2010). *Shadow and Double: Illusions of Identity, Presence and Absence.* Lecture given at the 5th Frances Tustin International Conference, Berlin, Germany.

Schellekes, A. (2013). Arid mental landscapes and avid cravings for human contact – Beckettian and analytic narratives. *EPF Bulletin,* 140–153.

Schellekes, A. (2019). Arid mental landscapes and avid cravings for human contact – Beckettian and analytic narratives. *British Journal of Psychotherapy,* 35(1): 91–106.

Segal, H. (1957). Notes on symbol function. *International Journal Psychoanalysis,* 38: 391–397.

Saul, L.J. & Curtis, G.C. (1967). Dream form and strength of impulse in dreams of falling and other dreams of descent. *International Journal of Psychoanalysis,* 48: 281–287.

Steiner, J. (1993). *Psychic Retreats.* London: Routledge.

Tolpin, M. (1974). The Daedalus experience – A developmental vicissitude of the grandiose fantasy. *The Annual of Psychoanalysis,* 2: 213–228.

Tustin, F. (1981). *Autistic States in Children.* London: Routledge & Kegan Paul.

Tustin, F. (1986). *Autistic Barriers in Neurotic Patients.* London: Karnac.

Tustin, F. (1990). *The Protective Shell in Children and Adults.* London: Karnac.

van Alphen, E. (1992). *Francis Bacon and the Loss of Self.* London: Reaktion Books.

Waugaman, R.M. (1987). Falling off the couch. *Journal of American Psychoanalytic Association,* 35: 861–876.

Weissman, T. (2009). Sleep as a psychic envelope – The patient's sleep during the analytic hour. *Sihot-Dialogue, Israel Journal of Psychotherapy,* 23(3).

Winnicott, D.W. (1935). The manic defence. In *Through Paediatriatics to Psychoanalysis.* London: Karnac, 1992.

Winnicott, D.W. (1949). Mind and its relation to psyche-soma. In *Through Paediatrics to Psychoanalysis.* London: Karnac, 1992.

Winnicott, D.W. (1951). Transitional objects and transitional phenomena. In *Through Paediatrics to Psychoanalysis.* London: Karnac, 1992.

Winnicott, D.W. (1953). From dependence towards independence in the development of the individual. In *Through Paediatrics to Psychoanalysis.* London: Karnac, 1992.

Winnicott, D.W. (1954a). Withdrawal and regression. In *Through Paediatrics to Psychoanalysis.* London: Karnac, 1992.

Winnicott, D.W. (1954b). Metapsychological and clinical aspects of regression within psycho-analytical set-up. In *Through Paediatrics to Psychoanalysis.* London: Karnac, 1992.

Winnicott, D.W. (1962). Ego integration in child development. In *The Maturational Processes and The Facilitating Environment.* London: Hogarth Press, 1982.

Winnicott, D.W. (1974). Fear of breakdown. *International Review of Psychoanalysis,* 1: 103–107.

Wolf, E. (1982). Flying – Some psychoanalytic observations and considerations. *The Psychoanalytic Study of the Child,* 37: 461–483.

Chapter 3

When time stood still

Thoughts about time in primitive mental states[1]

> Oh dear! Oh dear! I shall be too late. When she thought it over afterwards, it occurred to her that she ought to have wondered at this, but at the time it all seemed quite natural; but when the Rabbit actually took a watch out of its waistcoat-pocket, and looked at it, and then hurried on, Alice started to her feet, for it flashed across her mind that she had never before seen a rabbit with either a waistcoat-pocket or a watch to take out of it, and burning with curiosity, she ran across the field after it, and fortunately was just in time to see it pop down a large rabbit-hole under the hedge. In another moment down went Alice after it, never once considering how in the world she was to get out again.
>
> —Lewis Carroll, *Alice's Adventures in Wonderland* (1865; 1996 edition, p.2)

It is not only the rabbit's watch in *Alice's Adventures in Wonderland* that hints at the dimension of time, which will be one of the tale's themes, but also his constant rushing to get somewhere symbolizes time's linear arrow, the linearity that will contrast sharply with all the things that will happen in the course of the story, in which time, space and the logic of events proceed according to other laws of "time" (Perroni 2004; Colarusso 1979; Hartocollis 1983).

This other sense of time has preoccupied humans since the beginning of existence. The topic is vast and complex, but I have chosen in this chapter to approach it from two complementary points of view: First, works of art which aim to decipher the experience of time and capture its conflicting yet elusive qualities in visual images; then, clinical states in which time figures prominently, making the subjective experience of time an affect in and of itself (Hartocollis 1983) and serving as a window through which we can enter, study and understand other facets of inner experience. In my opinion, one's subjective experience of time becomes a metaphor for a more far-reaching inner reality, the layers of which are less accessible at any given moment. Recognizing this subjective experience of time can expand our understanding of these deep layers of the psyche and at the same time more easily create a channel through which the patient can be in touch with these layers.

DOI: 10.4324/9781003479482-3

Works of art which directly address the topic of time

Of all the many works of art that have taken time as their subject, I have chosen to focus on some that, at different chronological points, have confronted the issue of time directly and explicitly. First, Magritte's *Time Transfixed* (1938)[2] features a powerful juxtaposition of a clock, its hands pointing to a particular moment in time, though one cannot know whether they are moving or have stopped, and a locomotive which appears to be both speeding out of the back wall of a fireplace and yet seemingly stuck in that wall so that any forward motion is in fact denied. The picture's title itself has a double meaning: Transfixed means to become motionless – held still – or pierced through, as an arrow cleaves through the air. Thus we have the condensation in that one word of two polarized aspects of time: Time as movement (*trans*) and time as frozen still (*fixed*).

In 1990, the Polish artist Jacek Yerka, inspired by an Edgar Allan Poe story, painted the hair-raising *Twilight in the Nursery*, [3] wherein a suspended pendulum and various other clocks figure prominently around a baby's cradle, empty but for a huge egg, and the room is overgrown with a vegetation so abundant as to suggest that it has been taking over the room's space for years, dematerializing it. Yerka explains (in Cowan 1994):

> This is a painting which foretold the future. I did this piece right after the birth of my long-awaited son. It was intended to be a painting depicting the evening quiet in a child's room. Only the rustling of leaves and the ticking of clocks can be heard. At the time, I didn't realize that the pendulum from the ceiling was slowly descending, just as in Edgar Allan Poe's *The Pit and the Pendulum*. The pendulum touched my son on August 9th, 1993. The room has since become forever silent.

This is how Yerka presents the experience of time following trauma, time as inquisitor–executioner, who brings about death and leaves in its wake an affective experience in which, following loss, time stands stock-still, its flow frozen.

I will now move on to Darren Almond, an English artist whose works center on trying to document experiences of transition and duration of time while holding the spectator inside the very experience he creates. For *A Real Time Piece* (1996), he constructed a video link to his studio which displayed the passing of a 24-hour period, the only change being the shifting shades of light that fell on his studio as the day passed. In a similar effort, at London's Institute of Contemporary Art (ICA), he linked up to an empty prison cell to illustrate how slowly time passes for a prisoner, the spectator becoming a sort of prisoner of the work itself (Grosenick & Riemschneider 2005). For his work called *Meantime* (2000),[4] he built a huge digital clock out of a giant shipping container, which was shipped from London to New York in six days, with the digital clock showing the elapsing of Greenwich Mean Time.

Very different again is Hanne Darboven, a German artist who created extremely meticulous, even compulsive, art. Her main concern was to catalogue, count and organize time. In a series of works titled *Writing Time*, she assembled and organized dates from the calendar, finding mathematical laws that linked them together. She created vast surfaces and gigantic structures, painstakingly identical, which enveloped within themselves different representations of time – personal and social – as though in an attempt to preserve every passing moment, and thereby find a sort of illusion of control and lawfulness in individual and interpersonal processes.[5]

In the exhibition *A Matter of Time*, held in Israel at the Herzliya Museum of Art in 2007, Narda Alvarado of Bolivia presented a short video work called *Olive Green* (2003).[6] For this work, Alvarado asked a group of traffic policemen to block a busy avenue in the bustling capital city of La Paz, by lining up across it, each of them holding a plate containing one green olive. The blockade lasted only a few minutes, just enough time to allow the policemen to eat the one olive on their respective plates. Having eaten it, the policemen then left the road, and the traffic resumed its normal frantic pace. This humorous polarization displays the enormous tension between the pace of the individual and that of socio-political developments, as here the guardians of order turn into the disturbers of order for the sake of a private moment. The work emphasizes how the experience of time's flow stopping is so contingent on the context in which this stopping occurs.

This confrontation of different speeds and rhythms is taken to the extreme in the same exhibition, in a video installation by the Israeli artist Ohad Fishof (2005), titled *Slow Walk to Longplayer*. On June 21st, 2005, the longest day of the year, Fishof walked very slowly across the frantic London Bridge, so slowly in fact that, setting out in the morning rush hour, it took him 9 hours 43 minutes and 25 seconds to get to the other side. Fishof's slow pace, in stark contrast to the rapid and purposeful pace of all the other people crossing the bridge, was intended to mark the fifth year of *Longplayer*, a work of music by Jim Finer intended to last a thousand years. This piece has been playing since January 1st, 2000, in five locations around the world and is due to continue playing without pause or repetition until its projected end on December 31st, 2999.

Most of the works I have mentioned above illustrate, I feel, the primitive fear inside us that (linear) time is like a creature possessing magical powers, whose lawfulness and everlasting presence threaten to swallow us up. In my opinion, the anxiety of death awaiting each of us and traumatic events that change permanently our subjective experience of living often set in motion attempts to capture the moment, as though such attempts could make it eternal, and thereby deny the danger of time moving on to its presumed end. Some of these artists have gone the way of constructing devices to control the movement of time, as though it could be frozen or endlessly prolonged: They have constructed elaborate mechanisms for the organized watching of happenings in time or tried to meticulously organize, catalogue and find laws in human continuities and happenings. Some of their works focus on and magnify the contrast between temporal modalities and rhythms that exist between any two individuals, a topic which is of great relevance developmentally and clinically, as I will further explore.

Time dimensions in the clinical setting

In these works of art, the focus on time is at the very forefront, magnifying through artistic tools how their creators deal with personal and collective traumas, and with anxiety related to the flow of time and to death. In contrast to this sharp and obvious focus on time, in our analytical work, although our theoretical thinking is replete with concepts having temporal connotations (regression, recall, progression, fixation, repetition-compulsion, developmental stages, transference, and so on), we and our patients make only tangential reference to time, which remains at the periphery of our consciousness but not at the center of our thinking. The therapeutic situation we construct is also suffused with aspects of time: We work mostly in 50-minute sessions which follow each other at fixed intervals, each session a fixed unit with its own clear boundaries of time and payment, whereas the process as a whole is open and timeless, as though it were gliding back and forth on the axes of time without let or hindrance. In my estimation, the essential quality of the analytical process lies in our ability to be with our patients in a state of unfelt and unvoiced movement between different times, not in linear time but in a sort of suspended time. The power of therapy certainly takes place in the "now" of the analyst–analysand encounter, yet the experience of that present time is not only shaped and determined by the relations each of the participants had in his or her past, but in its turn shapes how they perceive that past and even rewrites it (retranscription). These *après-coup* processes (*Nachträglichkeit*, deferred action) which construct meaning retroactively have been described so well by Freud (1895, 1897, 1918) and others, such as Modell (1990), Green (2003), Birksted-Breen (2003), and Pine (2006). Thus, our changing perception of the past, together with the content and processes that each session brings into being, creates a new experience of the present which, in turn, serves as a new past for future moments.

It is my opinion that the analytical framework, by embracing a contrast of temporalities (Namnum 1972; Sabbadini 1989) and processes which develop simultaneously in different time strata, invites us into the fabric of our patient's time-relations. Sometimes it even spreads this fabric out before us, opening a non-verbal window onto a highly complex, highly condensed psychic reality. The way a person becomes aware of the dimensions of time and the way in which that person lives them provides a sharp, precise and unmediated mirror into the way he or she exists with themselves and with the other. It does so, moreover, in strata of the psyche that are inaccessible to verbalization, even to thinking. In my estimation, it is precisely when the issue of time moves to the center of experience as a separate and predominant aspect of existence that there and then occurs a disturbance in our continuous and natural transition between various temporalities, one that often exposes an inner rupture, often of a very early origin.

I will now introduce a number of clinical examples which will allow us to focus on time experienced as fractured, fragmented and meaningless; on experiences of timelessness; and, lastly, on stereotypical, ritualistic, autistic-like relations to time perceived as frozen.

The experience of fractured and fragmented time

Noga, a young woman of 28, sought treatment because of a lack of inter-personal relationships, an eating disorder in which binges of ingesting huge quantities of food were followed by self-induced vomiting, and a feeling that she was incomprehensible to others. Her life was very much centered on her-self and her different spheres of functioning, especially her bodily functions and her creative work, as though her life were a sort of closed circuit, with very little external connectivity. Relations with her family were few and far between: She was weighed down by the feeling that her language and that of her family were badly unsynchronized.

In analysis, Noga filled her sessions with a barrage of talk which I often found hard to follow. She rapidly established a rapport with me, its key ele-ment being an intense staring at me and questioning of me, as though trying to pierce me through and assess how far I understood the nuances of her descriptions, and in particular how far I appreciated what was unique in her. During the sessions, she would detail again and again the quantities of food she consumed, and gradually I became surprised by my emotional reactions to those descriptions. At first I felt deep revulsion, as though I had been stuffed all at once with a mass of stifling, choking, rotting material. Then, gradually, there occurred to me visual images from movies such as *La Grande Bouffe*, [7] but one particular image kept recurring: As Noga described a bout of gorging, I saw myself arranging the dishes she consumed in orderly piles, layer upon layer, like a waiter piling up plates on one arm. My great fear in this self-visualization was that I would drop one of the plates, but even more critical was the arranging of the dishes in layers, as though I were engaged in a juggling act. At this stage of the analysis, that self-image would be evoked almost automatically every time Noga embarked on one of her gluttonous depictions, but what it meant to me was very elusive and made sense only gradually. At that time, the central and most significant aspect of the inter-action between Noga and me was her desperate thirst to feel me thinking about her ("thinking her") and especially to hear me describe in words, as fully evocative as I could make them, what I understood about her at every moment of our interaction.

A considerable way into the analysis, Noga began to talk about a time in her childhood when she was suspected of being retarded (I should point out that Noga had excellent intellectual abilities). This suspicion was aroused especially by her silence when asked simple questions, which made people wonder if she could understand the questions at all or else be able to answer them. For example, if asked, "What time is it?" she would not reply, since she felt that by the time she gave her answer time would have already moved on and would be different from the time when the question was initially asked. (Likewise, when asked how old she was.) Later on in analysis, she recalled a game she would often play as a little girl: She would lie on the floor as though dead and would stop breathing, trying each time to hold her breath just a little longer, to prolong this imagined death. On one occasion, a doctor had to be called in.

As an adult, her main activity was photographing herself moment by moment, the photos following each other as closely as possible, as though trying to capture each second, to leave no gap in between. With these photos, she would create displays of self-surveillance, infinite sequences of herself looking at herself looking at herself.

Gradually, a few thoughts became clear for me. First, that her descriptions of her relation to time, as they emerged layer by layer in analysis, altered my understanding of her, as compared to the early stages of the analysis. From her difficulty as a child in answering simple questions and her self-doc- umentation as an adult, I could appreciate the depth to which she sensed time as fragmented, each moment existing of and by itself, with no sense of con- nection and continuity from one to the next, or between past, present and future. The way she experienced temporality revealed the depth of her frag- mented and perforated experience of herself, as though she were losing her identity in the interval between seconds. I began thinking that all the food she consumed was a means of creating an infinite, concrete continuity, a means of filling all the holes and gaps in her self-experience. My own self-image, as a waitress balancing all those plates, with dishes in layers on one arm, worked on several levels simultaneously: It embodied the sense of a fragile equili- brium in her world, and my own fragile equilibrium under the "pile" of undigested parts she piled/loaded onto me while I was struggling not to "drop" her; at the same time, the image built in me an orderly stratigraphic sequence, in a world experienced as overwhelming and devoid of logical sequence. Looking back, I think there was also in this image a degree of dis- sociation from the very feeling of overwhelming revulsion that I felt at times, as though the acrobatics I was imagining carried me away from sinking into something one could only escape by vomiting it out. Noga's pretend deaths served as a primitive means of coping with her sense of discontinuity: Para- doxically, this death, whose duration she held in her control, became an experience of sustained alive-ness because this death was her own sustained doing and its time was no longer fragmented. It created, on the one hand, the illusion of timelessness such as there could be only in death, and on the other hand, of continuity, since the experience she created lasted for a substantial period of time. Without revealing Noga's family background, for confidentiality reasons, suffice it to say that, unsurprisingly, it was this pretend death that created a sense of continuity, since it reconstructed, I believe, Noga's sense of death within her mother and in the mother's presence. This was a prolonged emotional void, the consequence of which was the loss of all sense of a continuous inner self.

At this stage of the analysis, as I came to a clearer understanding of my recurrent self-image and worked through various memories, it became steadily more obvious how much Noga needed to construct a continuity of experience *via me*. Time after time after time I recalled, gathered together, sorted out, translated, connected and made associations between one experience and another, one moment and another, between my reactions and hers, between what was happening in our present relations and her relations outside analysis or her memory fragments from early childhood. This wide compass of interventions served, in my estimation, to sew up stitch by stitch Noga's memory envelope, which for years had had such huge holes in it that it was as though her experience were composed of unconnected and meaningless shreds and patches.

Before I talk about some of the characteristics of such a sense of fragmented time, I would like to say a few words about the developmental aspects of the sense of time. Having understood these, we shall be able to better appreciate the developmental roots of fragmented time.

Developmental considerations regarding one's sense of time

All schools of analytical thought agree that the experience of time is a product of interpersonal interaction during the earliest stages of life (Priel 1997, 2004). Both the sense of duration and the experience of time as a process that constructs meaning by connecting inner to outer events are perceived as deriving from the ongoing synchronization, adaptation and transformation which gradually differentiate between self and other. We even have, nowadays, the fascinating notion that the first representations of time are created in the womb, through the first sensations of rhythm, constancy and regularity. Rhythm, in itself, is composed of sequences of presence and absence, of "is" and "is not," and so forms the primary basis for the ability to tolerate change and difference. From the gestational age of three months, the fetus hears the rhythms of the mother's corporeal sounds (her heartbeat, the sounds of food digestion – themselves varying according to the mother's eating rhythms) and the sound of the mother's voice and of other people approaching and retreating at different rates. The memory traces of these rhythms create what Suzanne Maiello has termed a "sound object" (1995) and constitute one of the first representations of the maternal object, the first representation of process and continuity. This constancy and rhythm form the basis of fetus–mother interaction and become the earliest biological clock that is absorbed in the nucleus of the prenatal psyche (Mancia 1981; Maiello 2001). After birth as well, sensations and experiences of rhythm continue to take root and expand, to now include the rhythms of breastfeeding, of stretching and relaxation, of breathing, of sleeping and waking, of hunger and fullness, of presence and absence, of being with and away from the object (Arlow 1986; Birksted-Breen 2007; Colarusso 1979; Fraser 1981).

Gradually, the chief vector of a baby's post-natal development establishes itself through coping with the lapse of time between the awakening of a need and its satisfaction by the object (Freud 1920; Bion 1962; Birksted-Breen 2003). The experience which this period of waiting generates depends on the object's ability to adapt to the baby's stage of development. In Winnicott's thinking (Winnicott 1956, 1960, 1962), during this time of unintegration, the mother's total adaptation to her baby's needs allows for a sense of "going-on-being," a concept saturated with temporal connotations. This total adaptation makes possible a developmental process without any sense of "impingement" that would otherwise engender feelings of severe fragmentation. In the earliest developmental stages, present and future are simultaneous, since the baby's illusion of omnipotence and the mother's consent to this make the wish for satisfaction co-existent with the satisfaction itself. In effect, this is a period of fusion, of timelessness. Gradually, frustration becomes possible, in doses adjusted to the baby's capacity to bear it. There come moments of waiting, which form the primary basis for separateness and thinking, as the baby pictures the object in its absence by (sensually) recalling its presence. Of course, the capacity to wait without being filled with disintegrating anxiety depends on the inner knowledge that there is a reasonable time limit to the period of frustration, that a conception of process and a primary recall of the object's presence exist, and that the first buds of the integration of past, present and future have emerged (Priel 1997). If need satisfaction at this stage continues to be total, some of the excitement inherent in the baby's expectancy fades and less recourse to object recall occurs. If, on the other hand, the waiting time is prolonged more than the baby can bear, then disintegrating anxiety sets in, beyond the baby's mental capacity to process. To sum up, in the terminology of Green (2003), this complex interaction between two others contains within it what he calls a "conflictual heterochrony": The temporal encounter of mother and baby includes the time dimension of both, and although the time of each contains similar elements (drive time, ego time, future time shaped by the prohibitions of the superego, the time of the encountered other), the time of each is regulated differently. Mother and baby are engaged in an intense negotiation with each other, the baby moving progressively towards identifying with its mother's time, while the mother regresses to identifying with her baby's wishes. Fantasy time regulates the interaction between the two when they are not together. As a result of the negotiation between mother's and baby's time, there emerges what Green calls "transitional time," analogous to "transitional space," which turns waiting time into a time of expectancy of renewed joining. When waiting time extends beyond the baby's capacity to wait, potential time turns into dead time, analogous to empty space, in which there is a "representation of absence of representation," of death, laying the ground for negative trauma. In other words, it is from such a state that there emerges that permanent experience of absence which destroys the capacity of expectation, and even the capacity to perceive the presence of the object when it does eventually arrive (Green 1999, 2003; Eigen 1996). In fact, the traumatic element in these states is neither the prolonged waiting nor being cut off from the object; it is the loss of the capacity for object representation (Botella & Botella 2005). Thus, instead of the mother–baby interaction engendering a fantasy of shared memory (like Anzieu's fantasy of a shared skin (1989)) and a memory envelope which holds a sense of a continuous self, stretching across individual moments and events, a perforated memory envelope riddled with holes is engendered (Enriquez 1990).

In Bionian language, in the primary stages of development, the primary representation of time is in the mother's psyche, which, by means of reverie, brings about a transformation of the baby's mental and physical materials (Bion 1962). It is this reworking of materials in the mother's psyche that enables the baby to wait. Dana Birksted-Breen (2003) calls this time "reverberation time" – that time needed for all the developments taking place within the mother as her baby's experience of present time reverberates within her and from within her. Thus, the mother digests her baby's mental materials in a sort of temporal spiral. It is this reverberation time that, little by little, enables the baby to internalize a primary sense of process and waiting.

Further thoughts on the experience of fragmented time

To return to Noga, what had formed inside her was an experiential world composed of an infinity of moments, each one void of meaning or of any sense of historical agency, as though she were wholly made up of meaningless particles of experience (see also Loewald's description of fragmented time (1972)). In my estimation, Noga's waiting time as a baby was as I have described above: Never in her life had she encountered an emotionally-alive object. Her waiting had become a sort of dead time, the same time she learned to reconstruct in her "pretend death" game, with the difference that, in the latter, she was in control. Her inner world had filled with that "representation of absence," a representation which led her to spend her time in innumerable rituals of painstakingly assembling and cataloguing details and memory fragments; in effect what developed was a narcissistic withdrawal and severing of contacts, as she created a world ruled omnipotently by her, where she seemingly had the power to kill and revive herself at will. But this ceaseless activity had not healed her lack of a sense of continuity and mean-ingful personal history, and that is why she periodically had recourse to binges of eating – to materially fill up the holes inside her. For some time, the essence of the therapeutic effort was for me to act as a sort of sounding board, letting the fractions of her experience reverberate inside me and, afterwards, in dialogue with her. In such a state, there was no capacity of symbolization, for this is a developmental achievement which can only be built on the ability to bear separateness, which in turn rests on the bearability of space between self and other, between the concrete and the symbolic. In my understanding, much of the therapeutic work in this analysis operated on a pre-symbolic level, which Spero (1995, 1998) calls "symbolification" and which lays the ground for work of a more symbolic character, able to move freely between past, present and future. For example, I would say that the visual image that emerged within me, where I was balancing a precarious pyramid of plates of food on one arm, had figurative potential (Enriquez 1990), and that all the effort I made to translate that image was a work of "symbolification," laying the ground for later, more symbolic work. During these stages of the analysis, I had to act as a breach healer and connector until Noga could develop these capacities for herself and her sense of frag-mentariness became less acute.

The experience of timelessness

I would like now to illustrate a completely different sense of time than the fragmented one which characterized Noga. Yoav was a man in his fifties who came to therapy out of the desire to cope with the relations within his nuclear and extended families, and to understand himself and the decisions he had made over the course of his life, in particular in his professional life. He was a successfully functioning man, with an active social life, successful in his work in one of the free professions, pleasant to know, warm and possessing a rich inner world and an excellent verbal facility. The therapy seemed to progress smoothly on a wide and easy stream of association. But gradually it became clear that there was a region or stratum in Yoav's psyche functioning on a much more primitive level and which revealed itself chiefly in his relation to time. Yoav would spend long hours doing nothing, not knowing clearly what he was feeling but feeling that he was living the moment and was incapable of moving forward with any sort of clear intention. The professional work he should have been doing would come to a halt, and he would spend long per-iods of time floating in a sort of daydreaming. In precise phrases, he described how, in his heart of hearts, he took pleasure in feeling that moment could go on and on, that the present would never end, as though there had been nothing before it and there would be nothing after it. In effect, he was describing a world of no future or changeability, a world made even more extreme by his daily drug use, which made this sensation of an everlasting present all the more intense. He also revealed that another aspect of this long-standing pastime was composing music, but of a deliberately monotonous drone, minimizing any sense of variation or transition. Listening to the music, I heard how his rhythms changed so slowly that the listener only noticed after the fact that he had entered a new melodic passage. (In another context, he told me that he would buy lottery tickets and usually not bother to check the results as that would spoil the pleasure of his ongoing fantasy of winning.)

The experience of timelessness was described by Freud as early as his 1915 paper on the unconscious (Freud 1915), mentioning that unconscious processes do not change as a function of time, do not follow any chronological order, and make no reference to time. In his correspondence with Romain Rolland and in *Civilization and its Discontents*, Freud (1930) also referred to experiences which lack any time reference – any sense of boundary or demarcation – as "oceanic." The experience of timelessness is known to all of us from moments of great emotional intensity, from orgasmic experiences, from religious experiences, ecstatic ones, or from creative activities; in all these we lose the sense of time and sink deep into the happening itself, cutting ourselves off from our surroundings and from other routines of the day. We remember these moments for their intensity, for the sense of power and energy they impart to us. But here I want to concentrate on states when a sense of timelessness is a frequent occurrence (O'Shaughnessy 1992) and where there is a degree of attraction and addiction to the experience, a sort of imprisonment in the moment, as in Yoav's case. Many questions arise as to the meaning and function of these periods. Their nature denies in effect that living is a steady, endless flow of time. This sinking into the present moment disguises a denial both of the past, with all its losses and traumas, and of the future, which carries the inevitability of death. Yoav's life, as it began to transpire, was riddled with severe losses, with which he appeared on the surface to be reconciled, but under the surface his addiction to timelessness revealed a severe and paralyzing anxiety of death and hidden components of depression, all concealed under a rich inner world and under his ability to describe this world with great vividness. His sinking into an endless present, reinforced by daily drug consumption, the music he composed, his floating and daydreaming, all combined into a manic defense against the threats of terminality, loss and death (Winnicott 1971; Loewald 1972; Birksted-Breen 2003). In this state, in which the flow of time is denied and the present is experienced as lasting endlessly without ever changing, the blows of the past and the threats of the future are equally repudiated (Pollock 1971; Hägglund 2001; Lombardi 2003).

We have here, in effect, another fantasy of omnipotence (Modell 1990; Bronstein 2002), this one engendering a powerful "oceanic" experience, whose key characteristic is the sensation of eternal fusion, of a sort which denies any possibility of difference, separation and change, and whose qualities recall the period of fusion between mother and baby in the first weeks of life, also characterized by a sense of omnipotence, as I described earlier (Winnicott 1956, 1960, 1962; Arlow 1986). Yoav's desire for a renewed fusion, disavowing all change, difference and separateness, gave rise to an interesting interaction between us: He would often imagine thoughts of mine as exact transcriptions of thoughts of his and would sometimes hear my words quite differently from what I had actually said, attributing to me the ability to guess exactly what he was thinking or feeling. At other times, he would interpret my movements in the room as setting up a total defense and protection around him. All these situations moved him strongly, as though for a moment the two of us had become one inseparable whole and experienced a powerful sense of oneness.

Sometimes this sensation took on for him the qualities of a *déjà vu* experience, as if we had already lived a given moment or he himself had already experienced the new situation in which he found himself. This was another way of denying changeability, another indirect defense against death anxiety, as if he were saying to himself, "You've already been in this situation, it is familiar to you and you have come out of it, and so it will be with every future situation, including your own death" (Orgel 1965; Arlow 1959; Birksted-Breen 2003; Rustad 2001). This self-enfolding in the present attained not only the quality of eternality but also blurred the recall of past events. In contrast to Noga, who all her life struggled to connect up the scattered shards of her life and invested every effort into collecting and assembling fragments of memory, Yoav lived in a constant attempt to blur memory traces, especially the pains of loss, and his severe anxiety of death. His deep-seated separation and death anxiety and his masked depression showed themselves also in the unease I felt whenever I sensed pressure from him to enter into a sort of prolonged state of nirvana, devoid of any possibility of emotional or mental movement, and where both of us profoundly experienced any differences in thinking as discordant, jarring. I found myself making an effort to stir myself into movement, to concoct a story, to look at the situation from the outside, and more than once, apparently in complementarity to Yoav's feelings of *déjà vu*, I felt moments of estrangement, as though I were not part of the situation. I suppose this was my way of freeing myself from the pressure to dwell only in a totally happy present.

This tension, between Yoav's *déjà vu* and my *jamais vu*, helped us construct the beginning of perspective on Yoav's life. However, this movement on the various dimensions of time was met by Yoav with anxiety, at once disguised by his intellect. The therapy became my constant search for ways to enable Yoav to be not only in a symbiotic state of total mutual adaptation but also to remember his past and use the richness of his life experience without being overwhelmed by depression, and to enable him to cope with the fact of his being separate, with all the pain inherent in this state. Recently, as part of his attempts to touch the death anxiety central to his perspective on the future, he described how although he still feels that he will not leave a trace behind him and will be wiped away with a completeness hard to put into words, he nonetheless also described how he felt himself to be floating on the surface of time, with time, as it were, a river carrying him along. This was, in effect, his way of describing how, for the first time in a long while, he did not feel himself to be stuck and cut off from life but instead felt a sense of movement and alive-ness.

The experience of time as frozen, ritualistic, stereotypic

Lastly, I would like to give a brief account of a third experience of time – that is, of time as frozen, ritualist, stereotypic, which is characteristic of psychic states having a prominent autistic encapsulation (Maiello 2001, 2004; Spero 1998; Schellekes 2005, 2019; Tustin 1986, 1990). Keren, a young woman in her thirties, came to me after a long period in therapy with another therapist who had to end that therapy because of her life circumstances. Keren could not really say why she wanted to continue therapy. She defined herself as being depressed, whereas my impression was of some sort of frozen inner panic, in which any attempt to cope was all but impossible, as it overwhelmed her with a sense of disintegration and intense anxiety. Married and the mother of two children, she had never worked in her life, and only extensive external human support services enabled her to function within the family. She was engaged in no sustained activity, other than preoccupation with her external appearance, and had no ambition or wishes for the future. As to her body, she knew precisely how it should look and what clothes she should wear and expended a lot of effort in buying incredible quantities of jeans from a select specific clothes company. The therapy began with her telling me about herself as though we were old acquaintances or as though it did not matter who her interlocutor was. Very soon she developed a strong clinginess to therapy and would come very regularly and exactly on time, so that my feeling grew that her sessions of therapy had become a framework holding her together, just as clinging to autistic objects gives a sensation of border and demarcation. The relationship between us was similar to the adhesive equation that Tustin speaks about (Tustin 1986), or a sort of pseudo object relationship in Mitrani's language (Mitrani 1994), in which the main characteristic is that of being stuck to the relation, with no real and alive interactions, no real sense of separateness and no real mentation processes going on. During the sessions, Keren alternated between, on the one hand, empty silence, as though she were suspended in time, in a motionless state, a void of emotional and cognitive movement, and, on the other hand, moments of very concrete speech, extremely repetitive and stereotypical, every statement being repeated several times with only slight modifications of word order. Her daily life too was composed of recurrent procedures and rituals. The contents of the sessions were very limited, mostly focusing on the immediate past, that day or the one before, and on some incident that had seriously disturbed her. Every such incident was expanded hugely, since it took place in a sort of limbo, aroused no thought beyond its concrete aspect, and was experienced as having no connection to any other event, past or future, as though there were no story or history to her life. Keren's capacity for reflection was that of someone who lived without a mental space, without the ability to relate to the multidimensionality of a situation. What she expected from me was orientation, to give her direction. Indeed, when I spoke without doing this, I noticed that she often took my words, whether I had actually said them or not, as an organizing thread, which demarcated and affirmed her existence. At any break in our sessions, mainly due to an absence of mine, she at once called up other therapists, as though this interval of time was an immense black hole (Grotstein 1990) rapidly sucking her in – yet she would immediately forget all this when we resumed our meetings, once again as though the drama that had occurred during the break had generated no history.

In contrast to Keren's experience of her life as lacking any coherent sequence and meaning, our sessions gradually created an external orderly rhythm which lent her a rudimentary sense of the continuity that she lacked. In parallel, my own experience of session time was hard to bear: For the most part, I felt as though time stood still, in stasis, where everything was known in advance; nothing moved, there was no memory, and the main continuity created was merely the sequence of the sessions. This was a state of emptiness of time and space, where repetition/cyclicality was the primary happening, where there was no third dimension, neither of space nor of time, exactly as described in autistic encapsulations by Tustin (1986, 1990) and Meltzer et al. (1975). The personal and family history that Keren could recount was also very limited, comprising the most one-dimensional perceptions, which only served to emphasize how vast and deep was the region in her psyche which had failed to absorb/digest the severe and extreme experiences of finding herself, for long stretches of time, not to be part of her parents' mental space. This absence of any sense that she reverberated in her parents' psyche began during her mother's pregnancy and continued on from there, despite the fact that she was much loved. This had made it impossible for her to internalize any sense of continuity of holding, of process. Instead, there developed a world of circular, ritualistic attachment, devoid of all perspective of time. This rigid attachment, to times, to persons, to things, successfully protected Keren, at least partially, from her catastrophic anxieties of annihilation, but one result of this lack of a sense of process was an almost total lack of internalization. After some four years since the therapy began, a new and exciting development is that she is beginning to dream and recall her dreams. For now, the dreams are experienced as assaults on the even scrim of her life, almost as if they were intrusive objects. Their recall and their meaning is, for the time being, kept to myself, while in the sessions Keren still brings up her dreams as if they were some "bizarre objects" (Bion 1957, 1958) – material she needs to get rid of and which apparently has no meaning or relation to herself.

Concluding remarks

With the help of Noga, Yoav and Keren, I have presented a tour of time as it can be experienced, across all its intensities and polarities, in some primitive mental states. For the most part, time is not a major part of our awareness, yet on occasion it becomes central and sheds important light on one's psychic structure. As I mentioned before, it is precisely when the issue of time moves to the center of experience as a separate and predominant aspect of existence that the disturbance in our continuous and natural transition between various temporalities becomes evident and exposes a deep inner rupture, often of a very early origin.

In my experience, deciphering the way the patient experiences time (and space) gives us an additional key to primitive areas of the psyche which do not express themselves in the usual verbal or symbolic ways, be they part of a highly developed psychic structure such as Yoav's, or of more pathological states, such as Noga's and Keren's. In all three cases, we are witnesses to the human struggle to save oneself from the dread of losing continuity and memory, and, at the same time, from the dread all of us have of meeting the traumatic parts of our remembered lives.

Epilogue

Paul Auster's book, *Travels in the Scriptorium* (2006), depicts a man, Mr. Blank, in a room – imprisoned or free, it is not clear – and remembering nothing as to why he is in the room or about his own identity and life. In the room are objects, each with a label stating its name – aids to identification and memory, as it were. Mr. Blank does not recognize the series of persons who visit him, except for noting the sensory qualities of their presence. For the whole length of the book, Auster plays his usual games with the reader's perceptions, as the reader tries, together with the protagonist, to connect up his fragments of knowledge and memory. It is interesting that for all his lack of memory of events and people Mr. Blank has not lost the capacities of thought and feeling, and he is capable, when asked, of using them to imagine and write a sort of book, a novel within the novel, about a man imprisoned because of an injustice he has committed against others. Auster, who across several books has struggled with the experience of loss of identity and memory, peoples this novel with characters from previous ones, as though weaving a tissue of oblivion perforated here and there with resuscitations which allow these selected figures to exist in the eternity of literary time, beyond the span their inception originally allotted them. Towards the end of the book, the reader begins to realize that the riddle of Mr. Blank is going to remain unsolved and that, together with him, we are going to be left in a space of not-knowing and discontinuity, yet at the same time, says Auster, though it is true that Mr. Blank is an old and confused man, he shall not disappear or die as long as he, Auster, keeps him alive on the page by the act of writing.

To my mind, this book illustrates Auster's effort, and others' (Borges and Beckett, for example), to find words and meaning for the holes in our experience, for our existential need to make disconnections and not remember (if we think of the concept of the toxic function of the memory envelope, as described by Enriquez (1990)), for those places where we fall into pockets of experiential blankness, as reflected in Mr. Blank's name, where we lose the continuity of experience and lose ourselves in the maze of time. I conclude that just as Auster in his writings follows in detail the fracturing of the continuity of experience and the draining away of memory so it is our call to actively accompany our patients in the work of writing and re-rewriting every moment of their lives, of the past *and* the present, and thus to fight with them the battle of building a better past for the future to come. This role of ours is not made any easier, since the phenomenon of conflictual heterochronicity, described by Green (2003), not only afflicts mother–baby relations but any human relation. Thus, the therapist/analyst must cope with the complex disparities between their emotional rhythm and that of the patient's, with the disparities between, on the one hand, the tendency to forget and to deny the meaning of time and, on the other hand, the vectors which push us to remember. From my point of view, these thoughts represent an attempt to move one small step closer in time and space to that region within us where we remain forever a stranger to ourselves and lose forever something of what we have experienced.

Notes

1 This chapter is reproduced here by courtesy of the *British Journal of Psychotherapy*, where a slightly different version was published: Schellekes, A. (2017). When time stood still: Thoughts about time in primitive mental states. *British Journal of Psychotherapy, 33*(3): 328–345.
2 This work can be seen at the Masterworks Fine Art website: https://www.master worksfineart.com/artists/rene-magritte/lithograph/la-dureacutee-poignardeacutee-time-transfixed/id/w-3991
3 This work can be seen at WikiArt, the visual art encyclopedia website: https://www.wikiart.org/en/jacek-yerka/twilight-in-the-nursery
4 This work can be seen at Wikipedia.org: https://en.wikipedia.org/wiki/Darren_Almond#/media/File:Digital_Clock.jpg
5 This work can be seen at Sprueth Magers Gallery website: https://spruethmagers.com/artists/hanne-darboven/
6 A few images of this work can be seen on page 3/5 in the following CENART document: https://centronacionaldearte.cultura.gob.cl/wp-content/uploads/2019/06/narda-alvarado.pdf
7 Marco Ferreri's movie from 1973, in which four friends get together for a weekend orgy based on sex and food consumption on to death.

References

Anzieu, D. (1989). *The Skin Ego*. New Haven, CT: Yale University Press.
Arlow, J.A. (1959). The structure of the déjà vu experience. *Journal of the American Psychoanalytic Association*, 7: 611–631.

Arlow, J.A. (1986). Psychoanalysis and time. *Journal of the American Psychoanalytic Association*, 34: 507–528.

Auster, P. (2006). *Travels in the Scriptorium*. New York: Picador.

Bion, W.R. (1957). Differentiation of the psychotic from the non-psychotic personalities. *International Journal of Psychoanalysis*, 38: 266–275.

Bion, W.R. (1958). On hallucination. *International Journal of Psychoanalysis*, 39: 341–349.

Bion, W.R. (1962). The psychoanalytic study of thinking. *International Journal of Psychoanalysis*, 43: 306–310.

Birksted-Breen, D. (2003). Time and the après-coup. *International Journal of Psychoanalysis*, 84: 1501–1515.

Birksted-Breen, D. (2007). *Primitive experience of time and the analytic situation*. Paper presented at the "Time, Timelessness" EPF Conference, Barcelona, 2007.

Botella, C. & Botella, S. (2005). *The Work of Psychic Figurability: Mental States without Representation*. Hove and New York: Brunner-Routledge.

Bronstein, C. (2002). Borges, immortality and the circular ruins. *International Journal of Psychoanalysis*, 83: 647–660.

Carroll, L. (1996). Alice's Adventures in Wonderland. In *The Complete Illustrated Lewis Carroll*. London: Wordsworth Editions. Originally published in 1865. London: Macmillan and Co.

Colarusso, C.A. (1979). The development of time sense – From birth to object constancy. *International Journal of Psychoanalysis*, 60: 243–251.

Cowan, J.R. (ed.) (1994). *The Fantastic Art of Jacek Yerka*. Beverly Hills, CA: Morpheus International.

Eigen, M. (1996). *Psychic Deadness*. Northvale, NJ and London: Jason Aronson.

Enriquez, M. (1990). The memory envelope and its holes. In Anzieu, D. (ed.), *Psychic Envelopes*. London: Karnac, 1990.

Fraser, J.T. (1981). Temporal levels and reality testing. *International Journal of Psychoanalysis*, 62: 3–26.

Freud, S. (1895). *Project for a Scientific Psychology* (1950 [1895]). The Standard Edition of the Complete Psychological Works of Sigmund Freud, I(1886–1899): 281–391.

Freud, S. (1897). Letter from Freud to Fliess, November 14, 1897. In *The Complete Letters of Sigmund Freud to Wilhelm Fliess, 1887–1904*, pp. 278–282.

Freud, S. (1915). *The Unconscious*. The Standard Edition of the Complete Psychological Works of Sigmund Freud, XIV(1914–1916): 159–215.

Freud, S. (1918). *From the History of an Infantile Neurosis*. The Standard Edition of the Complete Psychological Works of Sigmund Freud, XVII(1917–1919): 1–124.

Freud, S. (1920). *Beyond the Pleasure Principle*. The Standard Edition of the Complete Psychological Works of Sigmund Freud, XVIII(1920–1922): 1–64.

Freud, S. (1930). *Civilization and its Discontents*. The Standard Edition of the Complete Psychological Works of Sigmund Freud, XXI(1927–1931): 57–146.

Green, A. (1999). *The Work of the Negative*. London: Free Association.

Green, A. (2003). *Diachrony in Psychoanalysis*. London: Free Association.

Grosenick, U. & Riemschneider, B. (2005). *Art Now – Artists at the Rise of the New Millenium*. Koln: Taschen.

Grotstein, J. (1990). Nothingness, meaninglessness, chaos and the 'black hole': I. The importance of nothingness, meaninglessness and chaos in psychoanalysis. *Contemporary Psychoanalysis, 26*(2): 257–290.

Hägglund, T-B. (2001). Timelessness as a positive and negative experience. *Scandinavian Psychoanalytic Review*, 24: 83–92.

Hartocollis, P. (1983). *Time and Timelessness*. Madison, C: Int. Universities Press.

Loewald, H.W. (1972). The experience of time. *Psychoanalytic Study of the Child*, 27: 401–410.

Lombardi, R. (2003). Knowledge and experience of time in primitive mental states. *International Journal of Psychoanalysis*, 84: 1531–1549.

Maiello, S. (1995). The sound-object: A hypothesis about prenatal auditory experience and memory. *Journal of Child Psychotherapy*, 21: 23–41.

Maiello, S. (2001). On temporal shapes – The relation between primary rhythmical experience and the quality of mental links. In Edwards, J. (ed.), *Being Alive – Building on the Work of Anne Alvarez*. Hove, East Sussex: Brunner-Routledge, 2001.

Maiello, S. (2004). The lack of time and rhythm experience in autistic states. In Perroni, E. (ed.), *Time: Psychoanalysis and Other Disciplines*. Tel-Aviv: Van Leer Jerusalem Institute and Hakibbutz Hameuchad Publishing House (in Hebrew), 2004.

Mancia, M. (1981). On the beginning of mental life in the foetus. *International Journal of Psychoanalysis*, 62: 351–357.

Meltzer, D.*et al.* (1975). *Explorations in Autism*. Perthshire: Clunie.

Mitrani, J.L. (1994). On adhesive pseudo-object relations – Part I: Theory. *Contemporary Psychoanalysis, 30*: 348–366.

Modell, A.H. (1990). *Other Times, Other Realities – Toward a Theory of Psychoanalytic Treatment*. Cambridge, MA: Harvard University Press.

Namnum, A. (1972). Time in psychoanalytic technique. *Journal of the American Psychoanalytic Association*, 20: 736–750.

Orgel, S. (1965). On time and timelessness. *Journal of the American Psychoanalytic Association*, 13: 102–121.

O'Shaughnessy, E. (1992). Enclaves and excursions. *International Journal of Psychoanalysis*, 73: 603–611.

Perroni, E. (ed.) (2004). *Time: Psychoanalysis and Other Disciplines*. Tel-Aviv: Van Leer Jerusalem Institute and Hakibbutz Hameuchad Publishing House (in Hebrew).

Pine, S. (2006). Time and history in psychoanalysis. *International Journal of Psychoanalysis*, 87: 251–254.

Pollock, G.H. (1971). On time, death, and immortality. *Psychoanalytic Quarterly*, 40: 435–446.

Priel, B. (1997). Time and self: On the intersubjective construction of time. *Psychoanalytic Dialogues*, 7: 431–450.

Priel, B. (2004). The other and time. In Perroni, E. (ed.), *Time: Psychoanalysis and Other Disciplines*. Tel-Aviv: Van Leer Jerusalem Institute and Hakibbutz Hameuchad Publishing House (in Hebrew), 2004.

Rustad, A.K. (2001). No beginning, no end: The illusion of timelessness. *Scandinavian Psychoanalytic Review*, 24: 112–122.

Sabbadini, A. (1989). Boundaries of timelessness. Some thoughts about the temporal dimension of the psychoanalytic space. *International Journal of Psychoanalysis*, 70: 305–313.

Schellekes, A. (2005). The dread of falling: Between breaking one's back and breaking through. Commentary on Franco Borgogno's "On the patient's becoming an individual". *Psychoanalytic Dialogues*, 15(6): 897–908.

Schellekes, A. (2019). The dread of falling and dissolving – Further thoughts. *British Journal of Psychotherapy*, 35(3): 448–467.

Spero, M.H. (1995). Clockwork and the symbolization of time. *American Journal of Psychoanalysis*, 55: 3–28.

Spero, M.H. (1998). The emancipation of time from autistic encapsulation: A study in the use of countertransference. *American Journal of Psychoanalysis*, 58: 187–209.

Tustin, F. (1986). *Autistic Barriers in Neurotic Patients*. London: Karnac.

Tustin, F. (1990). *The Protective Shell in Children and Adults*. London: Karnac.

Winnicott, D.W. (1956). Primary maternal preoccupation. In *Through Paediatrics to Psychoanalysis – Collected Papers*. London: Karnac, 1992.

Winnicott, D.W. (1960). The theory of the parent-infant relationship. *International Journal of Psychoanalysis*, 41: 585–595.

Winnicott, D.W. (1962). Ego integration in child development. In *The Maturational Processes and the Facilitating Environment*. London: The Hogarth Press, 1982.

Winnicott, D.W. (1971). Dreaming, fantasying, and living: A case-history describing a primary dissociation. In *Playing and Reality*. London: Tavistock.

Chapter 4

Arid mental landscapes and avid cravings for human contact

Beckettian and analytic narratives on psychic void and its vicissitudes[1]

Introduction

The very function of writing can be a way of structuring and restructuring the chaos of experience, an "ordering, reforming, relearning and reloving of people as they are and as they might be" (Plath 1991, p. 272). Thus, the creative self-transforms into the shape of the artistic creation, which absorbs, changes and presents the self, living now in a different form in the artistic creation (Bollas 1999a). A recurrent aspect that fascinates me in various artistic creations (Schellekes 2005, 2006, 2019), and especially in Beckett's texts, is the discrepancy between the exact structural organization and verbal precision of the written text, at one pole, and the quality of the emotional state portrayed in the text, either a chaotic or a void one, at the opposite pole. Often, this discrepancy lies beneath the experience of the writer or that of the character portrayed in the text. In my view, such writings are fascinating, as they succeed in expressing intense nuances of the human experience that are frequently unbearable, unformulated and unspoken, such as a deep sense of futility, meaninglessness, formlessness and emptiness. In such texts, one can trace the writer's ability to immerse themselves into, and explore the deepest layers of, the internal world – their own and that of others – and at the same time the writer's striving and craving to express as piercingly as possible these layers of the mind. Thus, the final text in these writings, the end result of a very complex creative process, both gives voice to these deep emotional layers and simultaneously, by means of a very precise and geometrical use of verbal images and structures, may be said to create a protective shell (Tustin 1990); a shell that, at least momentarily, keeps the character portrayed in the text (or the writer?) protected from experiencing extreme fragmentation and loss of identity. These structures impart a sense of form, contour and containment which in extreme states may be lacking in one's experience. However, it is in no way my intention to suggest that such texts should be considered as a therapeutic means of dealing with horrors of the void, but rather that they enable the reader to reflect on the power of verbally expressing very delicate levels of our humanity. As clinicians, we encounter void states of mind

DOI: 10.4324/9781003479482-4

frequently, but most often they are not expressed directly by the patient, and many times we infer their presence mainly through the defenses used against the unbearable impact of the empty existence. In my view, the richness of texts such as Beckett's enables us, as clinicians, to find an additional vertex through which we can reflect on our own and our patients' unbearable and unrepresented states of mind. Though such readings cannot and should not serve as concrete therapeutic tools against the void, they do, in my understanding, enable us to contain and locate these unbearable void states in a space whose poetic beauty, humor, and sharpness of expression increase our ability to look steadily at such states, and embrace and bear what is sometimes an unexperienceable psychic void.

In this chapter, I intend to focus on the experience of the void, moving back and forth between the various survival strategies and protective shells employed in the attempt to "a-void" this experience (Emanuel 2001). I will attempt to describe two distinct types of defenses used against such arid mental states that are devoid of representation. On the one hand, I will focus on excitation envelopes, rebirth phantasies and secondary symbiotic defenses of an adhesive nature. On the other hand, I will describe the repetitive, overly controlled use of rhythmic patterns of thinking, language and movement that help one develop an autistic-like protection against the sense of void and loneliness. In both cases, one can notice the oscillation between the defense employed and the still pulsating need and craving for live human contact, however scarce it may be.

I will start with a short description of my encounter with David, whose numerous modes of escape from, and survival against, his internal void had no precise mathematical features, rather, they were flooding his existence with extreme excitation-producing maneuvers, rebirth phantasies, and adhesive relations.

Clinical case: Part I

David, a successful businessman in his thirties, came to analysis because he had long-standing extreme hypochondriac anxieties. Soon it became clear that his life was a never-ending attempt to overcome the nothingness of his existence, his inability to be alone, and a deep sense of lacking any form, direction or meaning in his life. For all appearances, he lived a normal existence, succeeding in his business and married with children. However, in reality, he had no meaningful contact with his family members. He alternated between intoxicating himself with anesthetic pills and stimulating drugs and accumulating vast amounts of medical "information" to enable him to create an illusion that he could control what was a formless existence, felt as if on the verge of physical and psychical collapse at any moment. As part of this attempt to regulate his body, he would undergo dozens of medical tests and subject himself to all sorts of dramatic experimental treatments in various medical centers in the world, each time organizing an extensive social entourage to accompany him. In addition, he adhered to whatever could give him an illusory sense of vitality: He had sex with scores of women, he paid "friends" to accompany him all day in what seemed to him as live enterprises, he occupied himself with numerous seemingly exciting activities that could fill his time, and when none of these was available, he would feel lost, confused, and terribly anxious, as if he had collapsed into a state of unbearable nothingness, not knowing what to do with himself and how to stay sane.

Gradually, a very sharp and peculiar feeling started to become clear for me: In spite of his strongly felt presence and good intellectual abilities, his talking had the qualities of a logorrhea, a sped-up and inundating talk with no traces of self-reflection and no ability to listen. I felt him as if he had no inside, no real contact with whatever inhabited his soul, reminding me of Meltzer's (1975) description of the autistic child who drew the two sides of a house on the same plane as if the front and back of the house were one, with no sense of space or three-dimensionality. David talked about various things that had happened to him between the sessions, establishing no real contact with me, giving me the feeling that each session was just a short stopover, to be forgotten as soon as the session had ended. Whatever he recounted was done in an extremely naive way, as if lacking any emotional meaning for *him* beyond momentary sensual or narcissistic excitement. In addition, his narrative had a quality of dumping of facts as if by so doing no thinking process could take place, either in him or me. He would often describe how successful he was at seducing women, how much his company was sought after by many in his entourage, even if he was simultaneously aware that all these contacts were actively maintained by him through financial incentives of various kinds. Though all these maneuvers had clear narcissistic and manic features, I came to regard them mainly as *excitation and sensorial envelopes*, which functioned as corks to stop up a deep emotional void whose main feature was an ineffable and terrifying sense of emptiness and meaninglessness.

Increasingly, David started to portray a sense of chaos and futility in his life (though lacking any clear awareness of what he was describing), followed immediately by renewed attempts to create or adhere to an illusory vitalizing object. Soon these attempts lost their soothing ability, and he became strongly suspicious towards most of his relations, declaring every other session his intention to make new and drastic decisions regarding his family and his social and professional life. In one session, he proclaimed that he had stopped drinking and using drugs; in another, that he would change everything in his life – that he would leave his wife and children and start a new life, stop frequenting women, cease all his social relations and create new and better ones, go to another country and start everything from the beginning in a completely different way. Each session he would describe how everything had already changed a long time ago, though barely a few days had passed, and it was as if all his sense of time was completely distorted. None of these dramatic changes really happened, but it became quite clear how much all these drastic plans of transmutation were imbued with phantasies of rebirth and renewal, which gave him hope for a new life, devoid of the internal vacuum in which he lived. Transferentially, he seemed slightly more relaxed and less suspicious in my presence, and for the first time, some months after the beginning of the analysis, I had the feeling that he had established some contact with himself and that I could, for a few seconds, reach him.

Around that time, an unusual occurrence happened: He found an orphan kitten and became extremely moved by its fragility. He did almost nothing else but take care of it, as if a sort of blissful and never-before-felt fusion had taken place.[2] He now seemed to be able to listen to me for a short time and was touched when I spoke of his gentleness towards the abandoned kitten, who needed so much of his care, a care he himself had so badly needed as a child. He became less embarrassed and less suspicious in exposing his vulnerable kitten-self to me, while I was careful not to touch him emotionally more than he could bear at that moment. Once the kitten had grown up and become less dependent, David felt deceived and lost interest in it. The vulnerable kitten-David self that had just dared to express itself could not stand the flooding sense of meaninglessness and unbearable abandonment that was reactivated by the kitten's decreasing dependency on him and by losing the too shortly lived "at-onement" with it. In parallel, the fragile intimacy that had just started to evolve between the two of us was soon replaced by suspiciousness, and all his quasi-sexual/quasi-social secondary-skin activities and omnipotent transmutation phantasies were back again. He looked puzzled and moved to see me trying to understand what went on in him, as if he had never previously experienced being present in someone else's thoughts. He even seemed to be curious to hear the way I interwove the kitten's growing up and his own deep and old feelings of abandonment. However, these moments of emotional exposure and intimate contact between us might have inundated him, or intensified the anxiety that the emerging feeling of togetherness might quickly vanish as soon as his kitten-self developed in analysis. I soon received a message indicating that he would not come to our next session because he was on his way to the airport and planned to stay in another country for at least a month "to check how things are there." He said he would contact me immediately after his return. Unfortunately, that was the last contact, so far, he had with me; he did not respond to any of my subsequent attempts to connect with him. And so, though apparently he left to stay in a different country to fulfill one of his rebirth phantasies, actually abandonment and premature separation occurred again, albeit with some role reversal, leaving me to experience much of what, I believe, had never been thought, understood or represented in his psyche. Thus, I was left alone to experience the pain, helplessness and emptiness one feels when sudden and incomprehensible loss occurs, experiences that I believe had been part and parcel of David's early life, when their occurrence had overwhelmed him with unbearable anxiety.

Following Beckett's interesting formulation that "… the work, considered as pure creation, whose function stops with its genesis, is consecrated to the void" (in Pilling 1976, p. 20), I perceive that putting into words this short experience with David has become the impetus for writing this chapter and constitutes my way of bearing in my mind and processing what could not be experienced and mentally digested by David. Moreover, it is also a limited attempt to consecrate this writing to the elucidation of the concept of mental void, and of some defenses frequently used to alleviate it, all the while hoping that the function of this writing will not stop with its genesis.

The concept of void – Some theoretical considerations

The concept of mental void usually refers to a psychic empty area lacking content, form, structure, meaning and symbolic representations, all expressed through images such as abyss, chaos, black hole, emptiness, nothingness, stillness. The evocative power of these images reflects the very nature of certain underlying, unbearable anxieties, namely those of falling forever, of dissolution into a formless state, of being emptied of one's own psychic existence and thinking abilities, or of losing contact with self and other (Winnicott 1962; Bion 1959, 1962; Tustin 1986; Grotstein 1990a; Mitrani 1995; Eshel 1998; Valdarsky 2015; Schellekes 2017, 2019). In all these states, what is common is a mental lacuna devoid of representations, conflicts and ability for self-reflection. However, when taking a closer look at these states, some significant differences emerge that are relevant to the present discussion.

Experiences of emptiness versus psychic void structures lacking representations

First, *experiences* of emptiness and boredom are present in relatively well-organized personalities, including affective disorders and schizoid structures. In this case, one rather speaks of Bion's "no-thingness" (Bion 1970), a passive void/an empty mental space, albeit with a potential to be contemplated and filled with feelings and thoughts. We speak here metaphorically of the existence of an internal container – however empty it may be – which has a definite contour and ability to absorb experiences in a three-dimensional mental space.

In contrast, in more regressed cases on the psychotic and autistic spectrum, in which no sense of a container exists, one's experience can be of a tumultuous "nothingness" (Bion 1970), subjectively felt not as a static emptiness or boredom, but as an implosive, centripetal pull into the void (Grotstein 1990a). This is a state of having no floor, no boundaries, and thus no internalization of a mental space/container in which emotional experiences can be retained and processed. Devoid of reflective abilities and internal representations, such a state is typical of the "black hole" phenomenon (Tustin 1981,

1986; Grotstein 1990a, 1990b), wherein the experience of chaos and meaninglessness is accompanied by the terror of being sucked into an abyss of nonexistence. Following this differentiation, I will focus on these more regressive states that are filled with the acute terror of dissolution that mobilizes intensive defensive maneuvers.

Second, let us focus on the origins of the lack of representations that is typical of this terrorizing state of *psychic void*. Tustin (1986) described the catastrophic anxieties that fill a child's psyche when it prematurely experiences a sense of separateness from the object, so that the self is torn apart from what was formerly experienced as part of the self. In primary states of undifferentiation, where self and object are symbolically equated, the absence of the object is felt as if part of the self has been amputated, thus being experienced as a black hole into which the psyche is in danger of being absorbed and annihilated. The autistic object, which so often functions as a palliative soother, becomes equated with the human object, and its potential disappearance creates the same terror as that of the (human) object. Thus, Tustin describes how sensorial maneuvers become a substitute for human contact, leaving one emptied of human representations.[3] Grotstein (1990c) took this view a significant step further, claiming that instinctual drives comprise semiotic signs that both herald the existence of an internal catastrophic state and attempt to regulate that state. Thus, intense sexual fantasies and behavior, as one can see in David's case, foretell the existence of the terror of falling apart and, at the same time, attempt to regulate this terror by creating a sensorial and narcissistic exciting envelope, whose aim is to blur the experience of nothingness and meaninglessness, which is felt insufferably when containing functions of thinking and emotional processing are lacking.

From a different theoretical vertex, Winnicott (1971) viewed the lack of internal object representations that are typical of the psychic void as the result of traumatic experiences such as overly prolonged absences of the object at critical phases of development, or too strong inconsistencies in the parents' behavior. These traumatic experiences bring about a decathexis of the object that finally results in a *fading away of the object representation*, making the "negative" the only reality. Following Winnicott's ideas, but with a different theoretical twist, Green (1986) connects between the traumatic aspects of the "dead mother" complex – the experience that "mother is elsewhere" – and the work of the "negative" (Green 1997); that is, the active involvement of the death drive. He assumes that the death drive is based on the assumption of a negative narcissism that aspires to extinction and which is an expression of what he calls the "disobjectalizing function"; that is, *destruction through disinvestment*. The disinvestment can ultimately be directed not only towards objects and connections but also towards the ego itself and all its previous accomplishments, so that the ego becomes "impoverished, disintegrating to the point of losing its consistency, homogeneity, identity and organization" (Green 2005, p. 222). To put it in different words, when the psyche is flooded with extreme unthinkable anxieties that are neither connected to nor contained by a represented object, then the disinvestment becomes "the ultimate defense against unleashing of instinctual chaos" (Green 2005, p. 222). In such extreme cases, the psyche is actively emptied of its representations, so that the internal state becomes a barren and empty one, which not incidentally was called "blank psychosis" (Donnet & Green 1973). In a similar way, Grotstein (1990c) coined the term "actual psychosis" to designate an overpowering state of anxiety resulting from the inability to experience nameless dread without ego disintegration.[4] The actual psychosis, according to Grotstein, designates an extreme state of psychotic anxiety before the onset of "blank psychosis," which in turn may be followed by a delusional paranoid restitution, functioning as the regulator and structuring factor in an otherwise terrifying void of meaninglessness.

Thus, in a schematic way, we may envisage the following sequence:

Actual psychosis $\rightarrow$ Blank psychosis $\rightarrow$ Delusional paranoid restitution

In these extreme states, the loss of object representations becomes the basis for what Green called the "negative hallucination" (Green 1997), where one is unable to perceive the object even when it is present. Botella and Botella's (2005) conceptualization of the relation between perception and representation is highly relevant here. They describe how something can be perceived only if it is accompanied and reduplicated at a hallucinatory level; that is, only if the perceiver can find the object through their internal search for the lost and absent object. According to Botella and Botella, it is this hallucinatory sensory quality of the perceiver that makes the reality of what is perceived evident. Thus, to quote the Botellas, "the perception of the world emerges out of the unpleasure related to absence, just as the representation of the real object emerges from the pain of its absence" (Botella & Botella 2005, p. 173). In this line of thinking, when psychic pain exceeds one's ability to understand and process it, the psyche is flooded by an excess of excitation that fails to be represented. In this state, what becomes traumatic is neither the intensity of a perception or the content of a representation, nor the loss of the real object, but rather the psyche's loss of the ability to envisage (hallucinate) the object, ultimately losing its representation. When representation is lost, one is also lost in the realm of negative hallucination, unable to perceive and be in contact with the reality and qualities of the external object.

Clinical case: Part 2

After this theoretical interlude, I would like to return briefly to David's case. What gradually became clear to me was that, from a very early age, David's objects oscillated between an engulfing, controlling and intrusive presence at one pole, and erratic absences at the other pole. His early life had no sense of coherence and continuity; he was moved from location to location, many times in the absence of any significant other. Facing this tantalizing and chaotic discontinuity, David was left not only physically alone but psychically in the realm of a black hole devoid of representations. He gave the impression, as I mentioned, of a person with no internal space, having neither any ability to comfort himself through a connection with internal representations, nor any ability to perceive objects, including myself, as having any real and meaningful presence. In addition, he had no abilities to reflect on his internal experiences, which would be a natural outcome of having developed an internal space for mental processing. Rather, he was flooded by unmentalized experiences (Mitrani 1995), which continuously attacked him through hypochondriacal anxieties that became a signifier of an ever-threatening emotional and physical death. Thus, instead of internalizing a "rhythm of safety" (Tustin 1986, p. 273),[5] David lived in a rhythm of breakdown-recovery-breakdown, where all the pseudo-medical interventions to which he submitted himself fueled his rebirth phantasies of becoming a new person, physically and mentally cured and reborn. These recovery practices created repeated painful situations, as if enabling David to re-experience the initial traumas, albeit in a lesser form and under expert external surveillance. The interventions did provide him with a sense of recovery and holding, but this sense rapidly faded away, as the care could not be profoundly perceived and inscribed in his psyche, since it met there the negative hallucination. The lack of representation, either through a fading away or through an active disinvestment, ultimately left David again and again feeling practically alone and overtaken by anxiety.

Rebirth phantasies as a defense against mental void

In this context, it is interesting to note that the very notion of rebirth refers to a rhythm involving disruption and continuity, as is also described by Bion (1992) when he talks about cycles of being murdered → being-all-right → being murdered. For Bion, when coming alive is simultaneously associated with re-traumatization, it is as if one is murdered every time one tries to come alive. As one comes alive, the object that murders life is intensely activated. As one puts oneself together, one also puts together the annihilating object (Eigen 2002). So, it seems that I and the analytic encounter became for David activators of both rebirth phantasies and the potential for re-traumatization. The small kitten itself also carried the connotation of rebirth and aliveness but soon became the murderer of that very phantasy.

Moreover, it should be emphasized that David's rebirth phantasies portrayed a notion of birth that involved neither pregnancy nor labor. These phantasies exposed repeatedly his lack of ability to bear the duration and psychic work needed for growth and development. It seems that the time needed for such a mental process would have been unbearable for David, since he would have perceived it as too threatening a gap between the phantasy and its fulfillment. This gap can be endurable as long as one has internalized enough good-object representations that would make one able to tolerate frustrations and survive the absence of the object. It seems that such a waiting would also have made David aware of his own lack, vulnerability, need and dependency on human contact, which were grossly debased by him, given that he controlled his dependency needs by purchasing human services rather than letting himself experience spontaneous human contact.

A few more thoughts about emotional versus structural mental void

The huge number of sexual relations and "adhesive pseudo-object relations" (Mitrani 1994) in which David was involved seemed to serve as survival defenses against his structural lack of representations. In this context, it is worth mentioning Lutenberg's (2009) differentiation between *emotional* void and *structural* mental void. The former relates to a *feeling* of inner hollowness or emptiness that is *experienced* emotionally and expressed as such, and is represented as an empty container waiting to be filled.[6] In contrast, the *structural* mental void, according to Lutenberg, refers to one split-off portion of the mind which has not undergone the structural evolution of the rest of the mind and thus has become a blank empty space stripped of representations. This structural void is understood as a result of very intense traumatic circumstances that interrupt the normal symbiotic continuity between mother and baby.[7] In such circumstances, a psychic abortion occurs, accompanied by terror, and a split in the ego is created, so that the evolution of this split-off part of the psyche is frozen. No psychic transformations occur within it, and the lacking object is substituted by pseudo-object relations, rather than mourned and represented. This type of void is usually not expressed verbally, as is the case with emotional mental void, but is rather detected as lying under compensatory defenses employed against the nameless terror which accompanies the structural mental void. Most commonly, these compensatory defenses include symbiotic links which one adhesively maintains with persons, institutions, drugs, or sexual objects. Such symbiotic links function as partial compensatory containers for the terrorizing void, keeping the person together. Any break in these *symbiotic-adhesive links* is not felt as a static emptiness, but rather floods one's psyche with unbearable terror, immediately enrolling again whatever defenses become available (such as "neosexual" practices (McDougall 1986, 2000), psychosis, or autistic withdrawal).

Returning to David again, my understanding is that most of his emotional life was governed by these dynamics: He desperately tried to rescue himself from the terror of his void existence, clinging to whatever incessant superficial relations and excitations he could find that temporarily calmed his thirst for contact, erecting rescue and recovery practices, and, when none of these were efficient enough, he would simply collapse into a state of terrible terror and confusion.

Autistic use of hyperbolically rhythmic movement as a defense against mental void

I would now like to contrast David's varied defenses against the terror of dissolution into the nothingness of his emptying mind with a different type of defensive existence. I am referring to the autistic use of rhythm as a main organizing and structuring defense.

If we take the myth of Genesis as a metaphor for the state of the newborn infant (Farhi 2008), then the first lines in the Book of Genesis become especially relevant: "In the beginning God created the heavens and the earth. The earth was a formless void, and darkness covered the face of the deep (waters) …". Thus, in the unintegrated state into which the infant is born, the infant will seize on anything that creates order and pattern so that the formless state will not be experienced as a terrifying and chaotic infinite abyss but can soon acquire some predictable, structuring and soothing qualities. Developmentally, one's rhythm of safety (Tustin 1986) includes oscillations between separateness and fusion, between tension and release, between binding and freeing, between stability and motility, between recurrence and change. These rhythmic oscillations which enable separation and differentiation to be experienced not as existential threats have a structure-building function. Even while *in utero*, the fetus experiences the rhythm of the mother's heartbeat and of her speech, alternations between engagement and rest, all creating first experiences of constancy and rhythmicity (Charles 2002). The memory traces of these rhythms are absorbed in the nucleus of the prenatal psyche and constitute one of the first representations of the maternal object (Maiello 1995, 2001; Mancia 1981; Schellekes 2010, 2017). After birth, too, sensations and experiences of rhythm continue to take root and expand, to now include the rhythms of breastfeeding, of stretching and relaxation, of breathing, of sleeping and waking, of hunger and fullness, of presence and absence, of being with and away from the object (Birksted-Breen 2009). The rhythm of presence and absence thus becomes a structuring element, a prerequisite for internalization of reliable temporal shapes, and of awareness of difference and separateness, which are essential for any symbolic and representational activity.

In various regressive states that are characterized by the structural void or by the black hole phenomenon described above, language and elaborate patterns, structures and rhythms, instead of being internalized as stable representations, are sometimes used hyperbolically as autistic shapes to ward off threatening nothingness. Thus, one can see that where under-structuralization of the ego core is predominant, an over-structuralization of its periphery develops, so that an outer rigid shell is formed against one's dread of dissolution (Kumin 1978).

I have chosen to illustrate this state through some remarks related to Beckett's writings, especially to his short play "Rockaby." In my view, a literary text often has the capacity to express and elucidate complex mental states no less than a clinical presentation, and sometimes with concentrated intensity, evocative power, and esthetic purity.

The rigid shell formation is particularly prominent in the linguistic and esthetic ways through which Beckett portrays both the internal void and the human attempts to survive it, such as through the use of *excessive rhythmicity* and *over-structuralization*. For Beckett, whose long-standing ambivalence towards his mother, mother tongue and homeland was well known, writing became a place to live. Thus, the *normal* absence of the object, which in Tustin's, Winnicott's, Bion's and Green's writings is a prerequisite for the development of thinking abilities, imagination, play and vitality, is different from the devastating absence portrayed in Beckett's writings. Beckett uses images as well as linguistic and narrative structures which are fractured and thus disrupt conventional expectations of coherence and narrative development. Simultaneously, all these images and structures are presented with a sharp sense of humor and irony alongside hard-forged poetic beauty, so that the texts both contain and locate the experience in a space/text where reader and audience can be in vivid and engaging, perhaps palatable, contact with the experience envisaged. Beckett makes experiments with out-of-body voices, stripping place and body of any familiar coordinates, as his characters dream of other roads, other lands, other homes. There is rarely anyone at home, even if there is such a thing/place (Ross 2011). He describes decrepit bodies and minds, enclosed in jars, dustbins, urns, thus using unsettling visual metaphors that stand for a deep sense of stasis, fragmentation and immobility. The human landscape that Beckett creates is populated by disembodied creatures that have lost their memory, their ability to think, their time perception, and whose linking and relating abilities are drastically ruptured. Thus, the disinvestment function working both intra- and inter-personally, which Green has extensively described, is vividly expressed by Beckett's "dulling" of the self: "What mattered to me in my dispeopled kingdom … was supineness in the mind, the dulling of the self and of that residue of execrable frippery known as the non-self and even the world, for short" (Beckett 1970, p. 18). In other words, many of Beckett's characters seem suffocated in a black-hole type of existence, wherein no internal presences can soothe the dissolution anxiety. This internal dread leaves Beckett's characters oscillating between flooded existential states and emptied out, blank existences. The former – similar to David's self-experience – can be encountered in his short monologue play "Not I" (Beckett 1973), where a female, huge, red, made-up mouth screams an unstoppable stream of broken phrases that act as a mirror of a chaotic and fragmented self-experience. The latter – emptied self – can be seen in Beckett's short play "Rockaby" (Beckett 1982). The static and lifeless existence that is presented in "Rockaby," as in most of his writings, seems to be alleviated by the use Beckett makes of structuring and hyperbolic rhythm-producing techniques. Beckett is a magician in his ability to sculpt the words he uses, the verbal rhythms he creates, the sounds he produces and the precise syntactic structures he shapes, all put together in an effort to give controlled expression to the experience of the negative.

The name of the play reminds me of the lullaby in which a baby's cradle falls from a tree, thus bringing together in one song both the image of a seemingly nurturing and lullaby-singing mother, that of a vulnerable dependent baby suffering threatening loss and trauma (as hinted at by the fall of the cradle), and that of aging decline and death in a rocking chair (Hale 1988; Keller 2002). The play is about a lonely woman, all dressed in black, who sits in a rocking chair listening to her own disembodied monologue pre-recorded on tape; the rhythmic and repetitive tonality and cadence of the voice matches her being ritually and mechanically rocked back and forth, up and down. The normative soothing effect of rocking – as with infants, who frequently rock themselves so as to achieve balance before being able to stand steadily or walk, or who are rocked by parents as a comforting means – becomes a repetitive and stereotypical type of movement in "Rockaby." Lonely and deserted, the woman is left in her rocking chair, craving and hoping for human contact with "one other, a little like herself." Though searching for "another living soul," one can easily notice the blocked, terrified and fixed "famished eyes" that are unable to perceive any other human presence, in spite of the craving for contact. Here we see again how the negative hallucination is of such intensity that perception becomes impossible and the empty window *panes* become a reflection of the woman's *pains* and inability to make any contact (Doll 1988), while the "blinds" of the windows become a mirror image of the emotional blindness and aridity of the rocking woman. The woman is dressed, so it seems, in what used to be her mother's black dress, when mother rocked herself to madness and death. Thus, the images of mother and daughter are condensed and superimposed (Simone 1988), annulling any possibility of escaping mother's fate and hinting at the same static and withdrawn existence in the daughter. Moreover, the woman's rocking can be viewed as a primitive body imitation of the type Gaddini spoke about (Gaddini 1969), through which the woman, by imitating her mother's rhythm, performs a ritualistic "autoplastic" effort to re-establish contact with a moving and soothing mother. The only words the rocking woman expresses in a repetitive but precise rhythm are, at one pole, "More" and "Living soul," as if asking to continue the rocking ritual, the only movement that enables her to keep the illusion of living and the hope to find contact and be psychically reborn; and, at the other pole, the words "time she stopped" and "rock her off," which express the woman's resignation from her attempt to feel she has an I/eye that can see and be seen.[8] The failure to encounter and perceive another (and, in Beckett's words, "rock her off/stop her eyes/fuck life/stop her eyes/rock her off") ultimately brings the woman into a fatal psychic retreat, thus drowning into the image of the very absent/dead mother (who "in the end/came off her head") from whom she desperately tried to escape, and, at last, fading in her own deadening existence.

I find this play fascinating both in terms of the void existence it strives to capture and in terms of the precise and exact structure of it; the play's rhythm of construction, repetition and, no less, sarcastic irony is built with both intense emotion and mathematical precision. As I mentioned earlier, the exactitude of this structure in "Rockaby," as in many of Beckett's plays, does not reflect, in my view, the balanced interplay between absence and presence or the reciprocal and rhythmical activity between mother and infant, which is necessary to transform bodily sensations into psychological experience; rather, it portrays mechanical and stereotypical features that function as an outer protective shell which creates an ordering pattern in an otherwise formless, disintegrating and alienated existence lacking any internally holding structures.

In retrospect, it becomes clear to me that the process of writing this chapter was catalyzed by my experience with David and by my (his?) need to keep him in my mind, in his absence, through writing and thus re-living, re-thinking and re-shaping our experience. In a similar way, it is my view that Beckett's deep personal experiences of primary object absence function as intense catalysts for his rich body of writing, while his apparently uniform and static texts become powerful emotional carriers and active containers not only for the extreme loneliness and disintegration of his characters but also for the anxieties that Beckett himself seems to have struggled with, and for expressing so powerfully and creatively the unthinkable and unnamable that each of us experiences. One can think of Beckett's writing and re-writing on certain themes not only as a repetitive act but as a derivative of a rebirth phantasy; each new text, though sometimes thematically similar, creates a new and rich self and affective experience. Moreover, it is worth remembering that Beckett's self-imposed exile from his homeland (to France) and from his mother tongue was followed, much later in his life, by his "coming home," by translating nearly all of his writings himself back into English, his mother tongue, thus re-naming, re-shaping and re-creating his texts/himself. Personally, I feel a great emotional debt to Beckett, a wordsmith who enabled me not only to name much of what at times feels unspeakable and unbearable but also to do it from a bearable esthetic distance ... and with a smile.

Notes

1   This chapter is published by courtesy of the *British Journal of Psychotherapy*, where a slightly different version was published: Schellekes, A. (2019). Arid mental landscapes and avid cravings for human contact – Beckettian and analytic narratives. *British Journal of Psychotherapy, 35(1)*: 91–106.

2   One can think of this fusion also as an attempt to negate and compensate for the spaces of separation inherent in the analytic pace.

3   Tustin, in a letter to Grotstein written in 1989 (Grotstein 1990b), uses the term "void" to refer to those children who never had any attachment to a human figure, similar to Spitz's institutionalized children who suffered an anaclitic depression from the beginning of life. Thus, she differentiates this primary void from the black hole phenomenon, where one has lost something which was formerly there: the (illusion of being one with) mother.

4 According to Grotstein, "in actual psychosis the 'nameless dread' constitutes (a) maternal failure to hold, contain and transform primary meaninglessness (chaos), (b) maternal failure that results in the decathexis (withdrawal of meaning) of internal and external objects, and (c) the spontaneous or spuriously evoked irruptions of per-emptory neurobiological disruptions, due principally to neurotransmitter disregulation and manifesting themselves as exaggerated mental states" (Grotstein 1990c).
5 "... a regulated and shared rhythm that provides the possibility for contrasts to be experienced safely together so that they can modify and transform each other" (Tustin 1986, p. 273).
6 This conception echoes my earlier discussion on the ability to bear no-thingness, if and when reflective/containing abilities exist, as opposed to the state in which, in the absence of reflective and processing abilities, any nothingness/meaninglessness is experienced as devastating and eventually filled with anything that gives a sense of fullness, even if illusory.
7 In Green's view, such a void is a result of a defense against object intrusion: "the *ego* disappears in face of the intrusion of the excess noise which needs to be reduced to silence" (Green 2001, p. 112). Relevant here are such concepts as "the invasive object" (Williams 2004); "the undead" (Sekoff 1999); Bollas's (1999b) "intraject" or Gonzalez's (2010) "failed births, dead babies."
8 It is worth mentioning that not even once does the personal pronoun "I" appear in the play.

References

Beckett, S. (1970). First love. In Gontarski, S.E. (ed.), *Samuel Beckett: The Complete Short Prose, 1929–1989*. New York: Grove Press, 1995.

Beckett, S. (1973). Not I. In *The Complete Dramatic Works*. London: Faber and Faber, 1986.

Beckett, S. (1982). Rockaby. In *The Complete Dramatic Works*. London: Faber and Faber, 1986.

Bion, W.R. (1959). Attacks on linking. *International Journal of Psychoanalysis*, 40: 308–315.

Bion, W.R. (1962). A theory of thinking. In *Second Thoughts*. London: Heinemann.

Bion, W.R. (1970). *Attention and Interpretation*. London: Tavistock.

Bion, W.R. (1992). *Cogitations*. London: Karnac.

Birksted-Breen, D. (2009). 'Reverberation time', dreaming and the capacity to dream. *International Journal of Psychoanalysis*, 90: 35–51.

Bollas, C. (1999a). Psychoanalysis and creativity. In *The Mystery of Things*. London and New York: Routledge.

Bollas, C. (1999b). Dead mother, dead child. In Kohon, G. (ed.), *The Dead Mother: The Work of Andre Green*. The New Library of Psychoanalysis. London and New York: Routledge.

Botella, C. & Botella, S. (2005). *The Work of Psychic Figurability: Mental States Without Representation*. Hove and New York: Brunner-Routledge.

Charles, M. (2002). *Patterns: Building Blocks of Experience*. Hillsdale, NJ: Analytic Press.

Doll, M.A. (1988). Walking and rocking: Ritual acts in Footfalls and Rockaby. In Davis, R. and Butler, L.S.J. (eds), *'Make Sense Who May': Essays on Samuel Beckett's Later Works*. Gerrards Cross: Colin Smythe.

Donnet, J.L. & Green, A. (1973). *L'enfant de ca, La Psychose Blanche.* Paris: Editions de Minuit.

Eigen, M. (2002). A basic rhythm. *Psychoanalytic Review,* 89: 721–740.

Emanuel, R. (2001). A-void – An exploration of defences against sensing nothingness. *International Journal of Psychoanalysis,* 82(6): 1069–1084.

Eshel, O. (1998). 'Black holes', deadness and existing analytically. *International Journal of Psychoanalysis,* 79: 1115–1130.

Farhi, N. (2008). In the beginning there was darkness: Images across the void. *Contemporary Psychoanalysis,* 44: 2–17.

Gaddini, E. (1969). On imitation. *International Journal of Psychoanalysis,* 50: 475–484.

Gonzalez, F. (2010). Nothing comes from nothing: Failed births, dead babies. In van Buren, J. and Alhanati, S. (eds), *Primitive Mental States: A Psychoanalytic Exploration of the Origins of Meaning.* New York: Routledge.

Green, A. (1986). The dead mother. In *On Private Madness.* London: Hogarth Press.

Green, A. (1997). The intuition of the negative in playing and reality. *International Journal of Psychoanalysis,* 78: 1071–1084.

Green, A. (2001). *Life Narcissism, Death Narcissism.* London: Free Association.

Green, A. (2005). *Key Ideas for a Contemporary Psychoanalysis.* The New Library of Psychoanalysis. London and New York: Routledge.

Grotstein, J.S. (1990a). Nothingness, meaninglessness, chaos and the 'black hole': I. The importance of nothingness, meaninglessness and chaos in psychoanalysis. *Contemporary Psychoanalysis,* 26: 257–290.

Grotstein, J.S. (1990b). Nothingness, meaninglessness, chaos and the 'black hole': II. *Contemporary Psychoanalysis,* 26: 377–407.

Grotstein, J.S. (1990c). The 'black hole' as the basic psychotic experience: Some newer psychoanalytic and neuroscience perspectives on psychosis. *Journal of the American Academy of Psychoanalysis,* 18: 29–46.

Hale, J.A. (1988). Perspective in Rockaby. In Davis, R.J. and Butler, L.S.J. (eds), *'Make Sense Who May': Essays on Samuel Beckett's Later Works.* Gerrards Cross: Colin Smythe.

Keller, J.R. (2002). *Samuel Beckett and the Primacy of Love.* Manchester and New York: Manchester University Press.

Kumin, I.M. (1978). Emptiness and its relation to schizoid structure. *International Review of Psychoanalysis,* 5: 207–216.

Lutenberg, J.M. (2009). Mental void and the borderline patient. In Green, A. (ed.), *Resonance of Suffering-Countertransference in Non-neurotic Structures.* London: Karnac, 2009.

Maiello, S. (1995). The sound-object: A hypothesis about prenatal auditory experience and memory. *Journal of Child Psychotherapy,* 21: 23–41.

Maiello, S. (2001). On temporal shapes: The relation between primary rhythmical experience and the quality of mental links. In Edwards, J. (ed.), *Being Alive – Building on the Work of Anne Alvarez.* Hove: Brunner-Routledge.

Mancia, M. (1981). On the beginning of mental life in the foetus. *International Journal of Psychoanalysis,* 62: 351–357.

McDougall, J. (1986). Identifications, Neoneeds and Neosexualities. *International Journal of Psychoanalysis,* 67:19–30.

McDougall, J. (2000). Sexuality and the Neosexual. *Modern Psychoanalysis,* 25: 155–166.

Meltzer, D. (1975). Adhesive identification. *Contemporary Psychoanalysis,* 11: 289–310.

Mitrani, J.L. (1994). On adhesive pseudo-object relations: Part I – Theory. *Contemporary Psychoanalysis*, 30(2): 348–366.

Mitrani, J.L. (1995). Toward an understanding of unmentalized experience. *Psychoanalytic Quarterly*, 64: 68–112.

Pilling, J. (1976). *Samuel Beckett*. London: Routledge and Kegan Paul.

Plath, S. (1991). *The Journals of Sylvia Plath*. Hughes, T. and McCullough, F. (eds). New York: Ballantine Books.

Ross, C. (2011). *Beckett's Art of Absence: Rethinking the Void*. New York and London: Palgrave Macmillan.

Schellekes, A. (2005). The dread of falling: Between breaking one's back and breaking through. Commentary on Franco Borgogno's 'On the patient's becoming an Individual'. *Psychoanalytic Dialogues*, 15: 897–908.

Schellekes, A. (2006). Writing as a protective shell: The analysis of a young writer. *Modern Psychoanalysis*, 31: 251–288.

Schellekes, A. (2010). When time stood still: Thoughts regarding the dimension of time in primitive mental states (Hebrew version). In Spero, M.H (ed.), *Ma'arag – The Israel Annual of Psychoanalysis*, 1, pp. 281–303. Jerusalem: The Hebrew University Magnes Press.

Schellekes, A. (2017). When time stood still: Thoughts regarding the dimension of time in primitive mental states. *British Journal of Psychotherapy*, 33(3): 328–345.

Schellekes, A. (2019). The dread of falling and dissolving – Further thoughts. *British Journal of Psychotherapy*, 35(3): 448–467.

Sekoff, J. (1999). *The undead: Necromancy and the inner world*. In Kohon, G. (ed.), *The Dead Mother: The Work of Andre Green*. The New Library of Psychoanalysis. London and New York: Routledge.

Simone, R.T. (1988). Beckett's other trilogy: Not I, Footfalls and Rockaby. In Davis, R.J. and Butler, L.S.J. (eds), *'Make Sense Who May': Essays on Samuel Beckett's Later Works*. Gerrards Cross: Colin Smythe.

Tustin, F. (1981). *Autistic States in Children*. London and Boston: Routledge & Kegan Paul.

Tustin, F. (1986). *Autistic Barriers in Neurotic Patients*. London: Karnac.

Tustin, F. (1990). *The Protective Shell in Children and Adults*. London: Karnac.

Valdarsky, I.H. (2015). 'Void existence' as against 'annihilation existence': Differentiating two qualities in primitive mental states. *International Journal of Psychoanalysis*, 96(5): 1213–1233.

Williams, P. (2004). Incorporation of an invasive object. *International Journal of Psychoanalysis*, 85: 1333–1348.

Winnicott, D.W. (1962). Ego integration in child development. In *The Maturational Processes and the Facilitating Environment*. London: Hogarth Press, 1982.

Winnicott, D.W. (1971). *Playing and Reality*. London: Tavistock.

Chapter 5

Daydreaming and hypochondria[1]

When daydreaming goes wrong and hypochondria becomes an autistic retreat

In hypochondria, we can frequently witness an experience of loss of contact and control over one's existence, including over one's body, and the ensuing need to achieve control over one's physical existence, through incessant awareness of bodily manifestations and of any real or imagined physical dysfunction. Kafka's letter to his father is most evocative of this experience:

> Since there was nothing at all I was certain of, since I needed to be provided at every instant with a new confirmation of my existence, nothing was in my very own, undoubted, sole possession ... naturally I became unsure even [of] the thing nearest to me, my own body ... I scarcely dared to move, certainly not to exercise, I remained weakly, I was amazed by everything I could still command as by miracle, for instance, my good digestion; that sufficed to lose it, and now the way was open to every sort of hypochondria.
>
> (Kafka 1966, pp. 89–91)

Kafka's long-standing mental investment in keeping the body safe culminated in a very special achievement: Some claimed (Drucker 2002), though it is still open to debate, that Kafka received the gold medal of the American Safety Society in 1912, for his outstanding contributions to workplace safety, and in particular the invention of the modern safety helmet, commonly called a hard hat. Thanks to his innovation, substantially fewer steel workers were killed in industrial accidents. His invention protected many people's heads, that body organ which Kafka himself could still use even when his body "remained rather short and weak" (Kafka 1910).

In a letter to Ferenczi written in 1912, Freud mentioned that he had "always felt the obscurity in the question of hypochondria to be a disgraceful gap in our work" (Jones 1955, p. 453). One hundred years later, we are not in a much better position, since it seems that the ambiguity and uncertainty inherent in the hypochondriac mode of being contaminate the study surrounding it (Lang 2007). I think that this state is due to much confusion that exists regarding a clear-cut classification of hypochondria, which stems from

DOI: 10.4324/9781003479482-5

the fact that it is both a feature in many psychiatric conditions and an entity in itself. Due to this confusion, many of the psychoanalytic writings on this topic (Meltzer 1964; Rosenfeld 1984; Bronstein 2011) have attempted, with partial results, to make clearer distinctions between hypochondria, somatic delusion, psychosomatic states, and hysteria. For the present chapter, I will limit myself to a few remarks regarding this theoretical debate.

The main clinical distinction between hypochondria and psychosomatic states is that, in the former, an intense and overwhelming anxiety regarding the body is frequently present, while in the latter, such anxiety is usually absent. Moreover, the psychosomatic's mode of being has been extensively described as suppressing affect to such an extent that their affective life has been described as being alexithymic (Sifneos 1973) or "concrete/operational" (Marty & De M'Uzan 1963), terms used by the American and French schools, respectively, to describe the poverty of affect and fantasy. Since the hypochondriac's engulfing but unsymbolized anxiety is so prevalent, hypochondria has been historically (Freud 1892) classified as one of the types of actual neurosis, a term used by Freud to include intense physical and emotional states apparently lacking psychic conflict, such as neurasthenia, anxiety neurosis, and hypochondria. All these states or occurrences are characterized by a high level of excitation that has not been processed, represented and transformed into digestible mentation (Mitrani 1995), as opposed to hysteria, which is considered to be the prototype of the neurotic symptom that embodies dense symbolism of an underlying psychic conflict, in spite of its physical appearance. Put in simple and phenomenological terms, the hypochondriac is deluged by body-related anxiety, while the hysteric presents a physical symptom, rich with symbolic connotations but accompanied by relative emotional indifference.

Though this debate is fascinating, it is much beyond the scope of this chapter, since my present interest is to focus on hypochondriac anxiety per se and its relation to excessive daydreaming.[2] Even in otherwise relatively well-functioning personalities, the hypochondriac involvement with the body may become so extensive that, at its limit, it can induce autistic-like withdrawals into a world of hypertrophied attention to one's sensations, where daydreaming on disease and deterioration and the ensuing torrent of anxiety become densely intermingled, creating a very painful and detached existence.

When working with hypochondriac patients, one of the striking clinical features is the extensive mental elaboration and detailed imagination about any possible harm to, or disease in, one's body, or else by proxy, in one's close relatives. One excessively indulges in self-observation and overvalues one's perception of the body, both of which are accompanied by the conviction of being ill and by disintegrating anxiety (Stolorow 1979) that is not part of a major somatic condition (Nissen 2000). The hypochondriac imagines how every little sign of physical distress and every minor symptom will lead to catastrophic and lethal consequences. Many times, as I have seen with several patients, the imagined scenario includes almost a trance-like state of mind, in which the hypochondriac gets carried away into an elaborate fantasy of how they (or a very close person) will be diagnosed as gravely ill, how their organs will deteriorate, how days and nights will be spent in pain and anguish while undergoing medical treatments and prolonged hospitalizations, how lonely and frightful such states will be experienced. These daydreamed narratives, when employed excessively, acquire autistic features, as the hypochondriac sinks into a world governed by sensations, getting more and more detached from their surroundings and wailing/lamenting the miserable imagined existence that will befall them. Though inundating anxiety is often present, in my experience, this type of daydreaming disease-related scenarios acquires many times an oneiric quality in which a visible contradiction exists between the frightening content of the hypochondriac fantasy and the affect and tone of voice that accompany the verbalization of this fantasy. In these instances, while imagining the expected somatic catastrophe, the melody of the speech and the affect expressed are not always anxiety-laden but sometimes convey a sense of being carried away into a land of dreaming, full of masochistic painful stimulation. It is important to note that the essence of the hereby described daydream fantasy is not always accompanied by death anxiety proper (though apparently one would suspect that, since most imagined diseases are terminal), but rather by a rich imagery of a state of being ill, of suffering, of the body being invaded by malady, pain and intrusive medical practices.[3] The masochistic component is evident in this imagery,[4] as the hypochondriac is both terrorized by their conviction of being afflicted by a serious disease and at the same time fascinated by, and immersed in, their bodily sensations; the hypochondriac is both anxious about all medical interventions while simultaneously soliciting medical care and procedures for any vague or specific complaint (Barsky & Klerman 1983). Thus, I propose that the hypochondriac ideation is a mixture of layers, some in which masochistic symbol-laden fantasies prevail and some in which the very sinking into and imagining of physical sensations becomes a sort of "autistic shape" that lacks symbolic activity, thus creating an autistic sensations-related enclave.

This state of excessive detachment from reality that is part of the hypochondriac ideation has ancient roots in the history of the individual. Before proceeding to additional theoretical aspects, I would like to relate briefly a clinical case that portrays some of the main points of the present discussion.

Iris

My relationship with Iris has been a very long one, with multiple and complex facets. For the purpose of this chapter, I will only focus on a few relevant issues that are pertinent to the topic of hypochondria and daydreaming, leaving aside many nuances that are part of Iris's rich personality and of our deep emotional relation over many meaningful years; although these could potentially enrich our understanding of her, it is beyond my present scope to detail them here.

Iris, a professionally successful writer in her thirties, married with three children, approached me for analysis due to terrible hypochondriac anxieties related to her eldest son, who was then a few months old. She was devastated whenever the baby showed any sign of physical distress, especially when he had any clear physical symptoms. Both of these were instantly experienced by Iris as grave symptoms heralding an incipient terminal disease or other physical catastrophes. In subsequent years, two more babies were born, and with all three children she experienced the same degree of hypochondriac crises, which would make her sink for days and nights into abyssal anxiety and construct elaborate daydreams about the imagined physical sensations and catastrophe that would befall her and her children. These daydreams included rich details of future scenarios in which her children would become gravely ill, would suffer immensely – physically and emotionally – would undergo painful medical procedures, and would slowly deteriorate until the inevitable end. The imagination was less concerned with the danger of losing the child or with death per se but much more with all the bodily sensations and devitalized states that would precede death. Alternately, Iris reacted to her own physical real or imagined symptoms with similar anxiety, richly imagining sensations and symptoms and how her children would become orphans, and how much they were going to suffer. She would calculate various ages at which being an orphan might be more bearable and less devastating, hoping that she would have the chance to live until the children had reached that age, so that they would not prematurely experience such a terrible loss.

In parallel to the extensive preoccupation with the seemingly diseased body, it soon struck me that this hypochondriac layer masked a very special relation to her own body, from which she seemed completely disconnected. Her physical appearance gave the impression that she had no interest in the way she looked. She was not physically neglected, but it seemed that her body was in a sort of suspended state, not really being experienced, except through possible disease. She showed little interest or pleasure in sex, hardly paid attention to clothes, to her haircut, and generally to deriving any pleasure from her body. Sometimes I had the feeling that she lived in a sort of emotional blindness to her body, which I suggest calling "a negative hypochondria" (paraphrasing Green's thinking on "negative hallucination"), so as to emphasize the lack of emotional investment in the details of the living and healthy body, and the lack of experiencing her body as alive and full of vitality. This dual relation to her body became more and more striking, as it seemed to mirror a very deep and old schism in her emotional existence, which gradually unfolded in analysis. On one hand, she functioned relatively well in everything that her life required, though most of the time being tired and lacking energy; on the other hand, she lived in a sort of daydreaming existence, slightly disconnected from the reality of her life, only superficially being involved with her significant others. She kept contact with few social relations, as her emotional energy was deeply caught up either in this "fantasying" existence, to use Winnicott's adjective, or in dealing with her extensive hypochondriac anxieties.

During our sessions, a very special presence of Iris began to preoccupy me. She was very devoted to the analytic process, always came to the sessions, talked, brought quite rich material, but often there was some lack of focus, as if she were not totally present, as if some disconnection from reality kept her in a semi-dreamy state. Sometimes she would slightly lose connection with time issues; sometimes she would not notice any changes in my office that were noticed and reacted to by most of my other patients; sometimes she gave the impression that my presence was a very important background but that she was not really in contact with me, on a deeper level. Moreover, for years she continued to be ambivalent towards me, as if never really knowing whether she was in the right place, regularly fantasizing that this or that analyst will certainly be a better choice. She would openly and frequently describe how excited she felt when she imagined herself with another analyst she might come to know or hear about, but she never really considered leaving her analysis with me.

The daydreaming of better places, better families, or better analysts alternated in the sessions with the description of her hypochondriac anxieties, which attacked her a great deal. Gradually, I became aware that in spite of the terrifying content of her anxieties there was a recurrent daydreaming quality to the way she described them, as if she were transported into a world of fantasy, with her collusion. Her tone of voice also became very often like a dreamy melody while speaking, slightly singing the imagined catastrophes, as if she also found some known but unthought-of gratification in the hypochondriac scenarios. At times, as if caught up in some contagious disease, I found myself struggling with a sort of daydreaming state, in which I was slightly losing contact with Iris, bordering on the sensation one has in hypnagogic states. The main striking feature of these states of mine was that I became both aware of and observed my daydreaming, while simultaneously I could hardly stop its sharp intensity. It is important in this context to emphasize that such a state has little to do with free association, as the feeling is of being taken away and losing contact with both external and internal reality.

I have detailed these nonverbal transferential intricacies, as they became a tunnel through which some of the historic roots of Iris's emotional development could be approached experientially step by step. From a very early age, Iris experienced her parents as living in their own slightly disconnected world, being simultaneously loving towards her and narcissistically and sexually immersed in each other. It seems that her parents had been unaware of the impact and implications that their stormy involvement with each other, and considerable disconnection from real matters, had for Iris's fragile existence and developmental needs. Iris learned to disconnect herself from her internal reality and from what was experienced as a very invasive and drowning presence of her parents, which was much above her abilities to process and understand.[5] Though such presence had obvious exciting qualities, it simultaneously became a haunting one. It seems that Iris developed all sorts of techniques of shutting out her sensory channels so as to become disconnected both from her parents' alluvial presence and from her own internal scene. During these times, she oscillated between excitation, anxiety and confusion, all eventually culminating in her need to silence her own senses and to become immersed in a disconnected-from-her-body state. She gradually developed her "fantasying" abilities, which offered her a daydreaming envelope that protected her from unbearable realities. While growing up, she became exposed to many separations and peregrinations, which created much instability in her life and which, again, were beyond her abilities to contain. Due to a precocious ego development, whose damaging effects have been thoroughly described by many (Klein 1930; Winnicott 1962; Mitrani 2007), and due to her high intelligence and wealth of abilities, she could adapt well enough, but she developed more and more strategies of disconnection. She would thoroughly engage in daydreaming, "fantasying" better parents and homes; she would deny frustrating or traumatic experiences, creating idealized scenarios, or would eventually retreat into her own body, sinking into a world of hypersensitive reactivity to sensations, a sort of autistic shell of auto-sensuality (Tustin 1990) that ultimately swamped her with hypochondriac anxiety. Thus, her exaggerated daydreaming and disconnecting abilities that had been established early in her life became both the carrier of long-standing anxiety and the means to deny it, through projection into the body. Simultaneously, to my understanding, by developing hypochondriac anxieties and by daydreaming catastrophic scenarios, she maintained a very faithful relation to her early objects: on one hand, she was invaded by unbearable anxiety (as she had been from a very early age in the presence of her parents), in the form of experiencing her body as under attack from a terminal disease; and, at the same time, she maintained her disconnected emotional existence through daydreaming, both of a catastrophic nature, such as in hypochondriac scenarios, and of an idealized fantasized future, such as when daydreaming of better husbands or better analysts. In addition, I would suggest that the hypochondriac anxiety also connected her with her formerly denied/suspended body, even if in such a distorted way. Moreover, her hypersensitivity to any physical sign became, in my view, a mimicry of a displaced-unto-the-body longing for attentive care (Granek 1989), so that the longed-for care administered by another was substituted by her own concern towards her body.

As it is evident in Iris's case, the early experiences of many hypochondriac patients are, to my understanding, frequently colored by an object presence which was experienced as either too exciting or too invasive, or a mixture of both, whether in terms of its inconsistency or in terms of overwhelming the infant with stimuli which were beyond its containing and processing abilities.[6] The parent's ability to help the small child with processing and representing the many sensations it experiences, the importance of which Tustin talked so extensively (Tustin 1981, 1990), is thus hindered when an invasive object is internalized, leaving the child in what she called "an agony of consciousness."

Even when the object's presence seems quite devoted, its possible invasive quality is confusing and overwhelming, as it usually lacks any boundaries, so that for a child's mind such an object presence is experienced as frightening and threatening to his separate sense of self (Arlow & Brenner 1969; Nissen 2000; Williams 2004; Skogstad 2013). In such a state of invasion, the normal process of projecting one's unbearable sensations onto the object is almost impossible, since the parent's ability to employ their alpha function is rather deficient, and the omega function (the reversal of the alpha function: The parental object projecting its emotional needs onto the child), about which Gianna Williams (1997) speaks, becomes the dominant one. When one is inundated by internal unbearable and indigestible states of mind and by external confusing and assailing experiences, one develops various emotional tactics, as we all know. However, the one I wish to emphasize here, as I attempted to illustrate with Iris's case, is the development of a detached, almost dissociative stance, made possible by the construction of a private imaginary world, disconnected from reality and, apparently, from emotional proximity to the invasive object – what Meltzer called a "pseudo-contact barrier of the day dream" (Meltzer 2009, p. 123). The infant thus learns to disconnect through building imaginary worlds, wherein it finds comfort and illusory control. In this context, it is not surprising that many times this excessive daydreaming quality about which I am talking generates, in later phases of development, fantastic scenarios of idyllic places and wonderful persons and relationships, all imagined as blissful, conflict-free zones of emotional serenity. These scenarios seem to mask a fantasized regressive oneness with the primary object, a "fantasized reversal of a calamity that has occurred and a restitution of an inner homeostasis that was disturbed years ago where a blissful unity with the 'all-good' mother of symbiosis" (Akhtar 1996) and infantile omnipotence would be possible. This fantasized reunion can become an excessive hope that, more often than not, creates heavy demands on real objects to fulfill this reunion. Such a state promotes the tendency of keeping reality at a distance, living in the imagined future while the present becomes a continuous source of masochistic suffering.

One can be mistaken and think of these daydreams as a version of the family romance fantasy, but in my view they are of a much more primitive and pervasive nature, as they often become slightly regressive cocoons that enable one to retreat into imagined worlds of better times and better relations. The blissful imagined oneness with an ideal object, which is present in these fantasies, is quite similar in quality to the timelessness experience (Hägglund 2001; Levine 2009; Schellekes 2010, 2017) in which interpersonal differentiations are blurred, just as distinctions between the time dimensions of past, present and future are blurred. When past experiences are traumatic and thoughts about the future raise the potential of re-traumatization by expected frustrations and losses, the timelessness experience enables one to temporarily live in a state wherein time freezes in a sort of illusionary everlasting present, thus negating the flow of time and the inevitability of losses and death. It is not surprising that many of the patients who tend to negate time dimensions and live in such timeless modalities achieve this through excessive day-dreaming, which becomes an efficient primitive maneuver of denying painful reality. I suggest calling such excessive daydreaming a "daydreaming envelope," functioning in a similar manner to the envelopes described by Anzieu (1985) and Houzel (1990) – that is, functioning as compensatory envelopes, when basic containing functions are lacking.[7]

However, when fantasizing turns excessive, it becomes what Winnicott named "fantasying," a dissociated addictive mental activity, keeping one in a state of distractibility and absentmindedness, absorbing much of one's emotional energy but not necessarily enriching one's ability to think, to dream and to be actively involved in life or, to put it in Winnicott's humoristic words: "nothing is likely to happen because of the fact that in the dissociated state so much is happening … and immediately, except that it does not happen at all" (Winnicott 1971, p. 26). The omnipotent satisfaction inherent in the daydream thus grows into an additional obstacle to active involvement in life, as most real experiences face one with one's own as well as with others' limitations.

The above description portrays a situation in which excessive indulging in daydreaming activity might crystallize an effective defense against invasiveness. However, things are more complicated, as one never totally relinquishes one's relation to the object. The repetitive need to stay attached to the object is ever present, even if in disguised form. Thus, when the infant/child's mind is engulfed by unbearable excitation or by erratic painful emotional experiences, many times an "attachment to pain" (Valenstein 1973; Aisenstein & Gibeault 1991) develops. Stated differently, rather than separating from the painful quality of the object's presence and rather than mourning this separation, in the hypochondriac's development, one encounters an adhesive attachment to the painful physical and emotional qualities that had characterized the object's presence. In other words, in my opinion, the imagined pain and suffering that the hypochondriac so extensively fears become, through the person's elaborate attention to physical sensations and imagined scenarios of disease, a sort of psychic retreat (Steiner 1993) into the body, wherein the imagined pain keeps alive the connection with the frustrating invasive object, who often becomes installed into the fantasy of the sick organ.

Thus, to my understanding, though apparently having been tormented by the object's confusing and invasive presence, one becomes the unconscious director of the hypochondriac drama in which the object that has never really been mourned and integrated is constantly kept alive through self-torment, embodied in the rich imagery of suffering and disease (see also Gutwinski 1997). This imagery echoes the invasive aspects of the original emotional reality, that reality which was experienced but has never become mentally assimilated. However, in the hypochondriac's subjective experience, they are the passive victim of the feared diseases, which act in this scenario as a threatening concrete and somatic reality. In other words, in my view, the hypo-chondriac subject vicariously aims at distancing themselves from unbearable emotional states, of both internal and external origin, by frequently developing, early in one's development, excessive, disconnecting daydreaming propensities, which sooner or later also become the venue for the daydreaming of somatic catastrophes. Thus, the body and the elaborate preoccupation with its somatic states could have potentially become a screen against the possible invasion of the object (Aisenstein & Gibeault 1991).[8] However, the hypochondriac's incessant absorption in their body keeps them forever invaded by anxiety, so that they never relinquish close contact with their invasive anxiety-provoking internal objects, with what was meant to be expelled from the emotional sphere. Moreover, the state of being ill may be viewed as a somatic embodiment of an unconscious search for a particular role responsiveness (Sandler 1976) on the part of the sig-nificant other/analyst. In other words, the hypochondriac's awareness of every slight change in the functioning of the organs mirrors how they wish the other would tune into them (Rosenman & Handelsman 1978; Granek 1989).

However, in my view, things are even more complicated, since the early object relations of the hypochondriac were never solely frustrating and painful but often an admixture of excitement and suffering, so that great confusion became the axis of the person's experiences. Very relevant here is Rosenfeld's understanding of the genesis of hypochondria as resulting from confusion related to deficiency in splitting mechanisms (Rosenfeld, H. 1958, 1964).[9]

When such confusion prevails, suffering becomes a source of pleasure while erotic life becomes a source of suffering. Frequently, the hypochondriac becomes addicted to fantasized suffering while having difficulties in enjoying real erotic life. The frustrations experienced in their erotic life become an additional venue for suffering and a potential source of additional detachment and retreat into daydreaming; this time, into rich scenarios of sexual arousal and romantic experiences with imaginary partners, who are fantasized as promising to rescue the hypochondriac from their real erotic life, which, more often than not, is kept under control and is maintained as a source of suffer-ing. In other words, one can see how the hypochondriac's confused link to the object as exciting, frustrating and pain-inducing is maintained in such a complex and imprisoning matrix of real and imagined relations.

Some clinical implications

The intricate relation between hypochondriac anxiety and excessive day-dreaming has, in my view, important implications for our clinical work. Since this relation is part and parcel of the internal object relations matrix that I have attempted to describe, it goes without saying that the main focus in working with the hypochondriac would necessarily relate to this matrix. However, I would like to make a few more points that seem important to me for the present discussion.

First, since the hypochondriac keeps such close contact with their body at the expense of their ability to be involved with objects on a deeper and more intimate level, the therapy/analysis should gradually create a protected space, wherein one can risk relating without feeling invaded and without needing to disconnect and retreat into hypersensitive listening to the body. If enough of the analytic work goes well, both analyst and patient can save each other from the danger of plunging into the excessive disconnection that often happens through the daydreaming envelope and other dissociative modes. This dreaminess and preoccupation with the imagined diseased body keeps one away from what is missing on the interpersonal level. In my analytic work with Iris, it took a long time until she could risk engaging on a deeper level with me, without needing to distance herself from intimate and intense contact. In parallel, it required substantial work on my part to reclaim myself back, sometimes with Iris's help, both conscious and veiled, from what seemed to be a partial sinking into contagious daydreaming.

Second, concomitantly with working on a richer and deeper involvement with the analyst, great effort is needed so that other relations, present and past, can enfold the patient in a more meaningful and creative way. Oftentimes, hypochondriac patients have neither emotionally digested the impact that significant others have had on them, nor are they deeply aware of the impact they themselves have on others. Relations are experienced in highly static ways, in which the object has no ability to generate new meanings and new realities, and consequently the subject's ability to be involved in dynamic and creative relations is hindered as well.[10] Since the detached, uninvolved relations are largely connected with an underlying need for a perfect and blissed union with the object, a union in which one can feel safe and omnipotent, the core of the analytic work becomes the need both to enable regression to primordial states of mind that have not been experienced enough, in the presence of an involved but neither invasive nor detached object, and, nonetheless, to gradually enable the patient to risk being involved in less than ideal emotional relations, while mourning the ideal object. Though it can be said that this is a main goal in almost any analysis, I wish to place special emphasis on these dialectics in the present context because – as already stated – the hypochondriac's reliance on daydreamed idealized future scenarios is so strong that it disconnects them from the reality of their life, a reality which is not necessarily as bad as feared.

Third, the hypochondriac anxiety masks a deep-seated denial of death and, by extension, of any limitation. The body is expected to be in a perfect state forever, with no weakness or ailment, as if one can experience absolute somatic security and, by proxy, absolute emotional stability. These features not only become a major part of the excessive daydreaming activity but also of the need to live in a timeless modality, wherein limits and terminality are denied. This denial may turn into a major issue in analysis, where time and limitations are an intrinsic part of the analytic texture. In other words, repeated attention should be paid to the various tactics employed by the hypochondriac to deny the flow of time and of aging, whether in life or in analysis. Moreover, since the hypochondriac anxiety is also a way of installing an imagined control over the body, there is great need to consolidate the hypochondriac's ability to tolerate uncertainty and, specifically, to bear a body that does not stand up to the patient's idealized expectations,[11] all this without their experiencing a complete lack of control, agony and helplessness.

Fourth, if analytic work can progress well enough, it is my understanding that the hypochondriac will gradually substitute their hypersensitive attention to the body with more mature, verbal means, so that their abilities to process emotional experiences will not be channeled into the body but will become part of one's matrix of internal and external relations. This, of course, necessitates a great deal of thinking and verbalizing on the part of the analyst, especially so since the hypochondriac's tendency is to blur and disconnect from emotional life, via hypochondriac anxiety or the daydreaming envelope.

Fifth, as I mentioned before, the hypochondriac anxiety and intensified attention to various parts of the body are by and large a distorted way to be in contact with a body that is not experienced as alive. Thus, the feared pain or disease, in this or that organ, becomes a mapping-the-body device, through imagined pain. To the extent that the hypochondriac can become more connected to their feelings and to their live body, including, needless to say, their sexuality, there is great chance that the contact with the body can be experienced as a source of pleasure, rather than as an imagined disease. Consequently, the more the hypochondriac can be in touch with and contain the vitality of their body, the less prominent will be the need to use hypochondriac anxiety as the main venue for contact with an otherwise suspended body,[12] a state which I have called *negative hypochondria*. In the analysis with Iris, extensive work had to be done so that she could progressively get in touch with her body, with her sexuality, and gradually she became more and more alive and full of vitality. Her ability to experience desire and to enjoy sexual relations increased immensely, even if many times her desires were still part of fantasies about idealized and unobtainable partners. The more Iris became connected on a deeper level to me and to her body, the less intense and less frequent were her hypochondriac anxieties.

Sixth, though hypochondria was originally considered a "toxic damming up of libido linked to a narcissistic regression" (Broden & Myers 1981; Freud 1914), one can think of unconscious conflictual issues underlying the hypochondriac symptom, such as unconscious beating and torture fantasies, related to denied hostility towards important objects (Broden & Myers 1981), or to early traumatic auditory primal scene experiences (Niederland 1958); unconscious fantasies of an internal persecutor playing the function of a concretely repressed superego (Arlow & Brenner 1969); or else displacement of castration anxiety into fears of becoming ill or altered (Fenichel 1945). It is not my intention to elaborate here on these possible underlying unconscious dynamics, but it is important to note their relevance, since they all raise the idea of the denial of, and inability to deal with, aggression that is so often part of the deflection that the hypochondriac anxiety enables. Consequently, the need to enable the hypochondriac to be exposed to their aggressive parts without fearing either destroying or being destroyed is of great relevance. Needless to say, this might have a great impact on lessening the masochistic attachment to pain, which I discussed above.

Seventh, a great deal of tolerance and self-containment, or containment by a significant other, are needed when working with the hypochondriac patient, since their catastrophic anxieties can be of such magnitude as to incur the analyst's need to defend themselves from what might sometimes be experienced as a potential physical and emotional flood. It is my belief that writing this chapter is a vicarious way of maintaining an analytic stance when facing such a deluge, as I have frequently experienced with some of my hypochondriac patients.

Thinking back on Kafka, whose hypochondria was as strong as his creativity, and whose writings were saved only partially by his close friend, Max Brod, against Kafka's enjoinder to have them destroyed after his death, I would like to conclude with the lines that Freud quotes in his paper *On Narcissism* (Freud 1914), from the last stanza of Heinrich Heine's Seven 'Songs of Creation,' in which he wonders about the act of creation: "Illness was no doubt the final cause of the whole urge to create. By creating, I could recover; by creating, I became healthy." Unfortunately, neither Kafka nor Molière, who died on stage while taking part in his play "Le Malade Imaginaire" (The Imaginary Invalid), were saved, in the concrete sense, by the act of creation. Maybe they could have been saved from an untimely death had they experienced Freud's saying that "a strong egoism is a protection against falling ill, but in the last resort we must begin to love in order to not fall ill, and we are bound to fall ill if, in consequence of frustration, we are unable to love." But that is also doubtful, since if love or meaningful relations are not experienced "as their own reward, but as a necessary evil, to be swallowed despite its unpleasant taste, like a spoonful of medicinal tonic" (Lang 2007, p. 8), then I wonder to what extent love can have healing properties. One hundred years after Freud's *On Narcissism*, I think we are still left with a lot to think about when we live the dramas of our patients who fight their dread of becoming ill and, even more, their dread of being fully alive.

Notes

1 An earlier version of this chapter was published in: Schellekes, A. (2017). Daydreaming and hypochondria. In Levine, H. & Power, D. (ed.). *Engaging Primitive Anxieties of the Emerging Self: The Legacy of Frances Tustin*. London: Karnac. The paper is published here with the kind permission of Karnac Books.

   Schellekes, A. (2019). Day dreaming and hypochondria: When day dreaming goes wrong and hypochondria becomes an autistic retreat. *European Psychoanalytical Federation Bulletin*, 73: 140–153.

2 When I speak of anxiety in this context, I try to limit myself to conditions in which hypochondria neither achieves the status of a delusion, nor is it part of an organic disease, whether psychosomatic or not, but is nevertheless extremely disabling for one's ability to live physically and emotionally.

3 Of course, this rich imagery of illness details can camouflage an underlying extreme death anxiety, which can thus be blurred or even denied. Very intense death anxiety is even more unbearable, as it is frequently considered to be a result of a failure to internalize the containing/protective functions of the object, so that any disturbing or threatening situation becomes the harbinger of impending death. The extreme fear of death is thus equated in the internal grammar with the experience of a collapse of defenses and regression to the total, infantile helplessness when the omnipotent parental figures had been emotionally unavailable (Starčević 1989).

4 See also Rosenman (1981), who conceptualizes hypochondriacal concerns as manifestations of psychic masochism, wherein anxiety is a form of punishment for bad wishes; and also Aisenstein and Gibeault (1991), who discuss the role played by the hypercathexis of pain in hypochondriac anxiety.

5 Though it is not clear to what extent we witness here an "objective memory," or a retroactively fantasized occurrence, or a combination thereof, what is evident is the invasive quality of this emotional entity. See Spero's (1990) extensive discussion on these topics, which is of great relevance here.

6 The invasive object is a term that was introduced by Paul Williams (2004) to describe conditions in which the infantile self becomes amalgamated with sequelae of uncontained projections and with the projective activity of the object that leave the infant in a state of emotional turbulence and confusion, which in turn threaten its very sense of self. The individual who has incorporated an invasive object is likely to feel unstable, depleted of personal meaning and occupied or haunted by unidentifiable bodily perceptions. The infant's body is implicated in the trauma, in that it carries the status of a primary object to which the infant relates, and which can become installed as an internal object, thus inducing one to "invite" invasion as a sort of identification with invasiveness. Williams also proposed distinguishing between intrusive and invasive objects. Intrusive objects tend to be motivated by a need to occupy or control the subject for reasons that can include parasitism and sadism. Invasive objects, on the other hand, seek primarily to expel unbearable, infantile conflicts using, for the most part, excessive projective mechanisms. Expulsion is compulsive and violent, but it does not appear to strive to control or become a feature of the subject in the same way, as its aim is to mold a repository for evacuation prior to a retreat to a position of pathological narcissism.

7 In normal development, though fantasizing is a less mature mode of experiencing, expressing and modulating inner experience than abstract and symbolic thinking is, it is nevertheless an important and creative means on various levels. To name just a few: It may help with processing inner and outer experiences (Sugarman 2008); it aids one in tolerating the object's absence, thus constituting a midpoint in the process of internalization; and it enables one to express ambitions and to anticipate important personal events (Lussheimer 1954).

8 This is even more relevant in extreme cases that border somatic delusions, wherein the hypochondriac aims to expel the diseased parts of their body into which their unbearable emotional experiences have been deposited (Rosenfeld 1984).

9 In Rosenfeld's understanding, it is the hypochondriac's mixture of libidinal and aggressive impulses that intensifies confusional anxieties (confusion between self and object, love and aggression, between pleasure and pain), which in turn generate excessive splitting mechanisms so as to get rid of the confusional anxieties. These are first projected into the external world to be later on re-introjected, but

this re-introjection is experienced as a violent and invasive intrusion that threatens to spread everywhere (Nissen 2000). The absorption of these projections into the body attempts to diminish the emotional threat by keeping it out of the mental sphere, by displacing it into the body, thus generating the hypochondriac anxiety.

10 I am grateful to the late Neville Symington for the generative dialogue we had on these matters (Symington 2014).

11 See also Starčević's (1989) discussion on narcissism and hypochondriasis.

12 In this context, it is relevant to consider Ferrari's (2004) and Lombardi's (2002, 2010) emphasis that in analysis with patients disconnected from their body it is necessary to work on the vertical axis – that is, on one's relation to one's body, as opposed to the common emphasis on the horizontal axis – that is, on transference interpretations.

References

Aisenstein, M. & Gibeault, A. (1991). The work of hypochondria – A contribution to the study of the specificity of hypochondria, in particular in relation to hysterical conversion and organic disease. *International Journal Psychoanalysis*, 72: 669–680.

Akhtar, S. (1996). "Someday ..." and "If Only ..." Fantasies: Pathological optimism and inordinate nostalgia as related forms of idealization. Journal of the American Psychoanalytic Association, 44: 723–753.

Anzieu, D. (1985). *The Skin Ego*. New Haven and London: Yale University Press, 1989.

Arlow, J.A. & Brenner, C. (1969). The psychopathology of the psychoses: A proposed revision. *International Journal of Psychoanalysis*, 50: 5–14.

Barsky, A.J. & Klerman, G.L. (1983). Overview: Hypochondriasis, bodily complaints and somatic styles. *American Journal of Psychiatry*, 140: 273–283.

Broden, A.R. & Myers, W.A. (1981). Hypochondriacal symptoms as derivatives of unconscious fantasies of being beaten or tortured. *Journal of the American Psychoanalytic Association*, 29: 535–557.

Bronstein, C. (2011). On psychosomatics: The search of meaning. *International Journal of Psychoanalysis*, 92: 173–195.

Drucker, P.F. (2002). *Managing in the New Society*. New York: Truman Talley.

Fenichel, O. (1945). *The Psychoanalytic Theory of Neurosis*. New York: Norton.

Ferrari, A.B. (2004). *From the Eclipse of the Body to the Dawn of Thought*. London: Free Association Books.

Freud, S. (1892). *Draft B from Extracts from the Fliess Papers*. The Standard Edition of the Complete Psychological Works of Sigmund Freud, I(1886–1899): 179–184.

Freud, S. (1914). *On Narcissism*. The Standard Edition of the Complete Psychological Works of Sigmund Freud, 14(1914–1916): 67–102.

Granek, M. (1989). Hypochondriasis, acting-out and counteracting-out. *British Journal of Medical Psychology*, 62: 257–264.

Gutwinski, J. (1997). Hypochondria versus the relation to the object. *International Journal of Psychoanalysis*, 78: 53–68.

Hägglund, T. (2001). Timelessness as a positive and negative experience. *Scandinavian Psychoanalytic Review*, 24: 83–92.

Houzel, D. (1990). The concept of psychic envelope. In Anzieu, D. (ed.), *Psychic Envelopes*. London: Karnac, 1990.

Jones, E. (1955). *Sigmund Freud Life and Work, Volume Two: Years of Maturity 1901–1919*. London: The Hogarth Press, pp. 1–507.

Kafka, F. (1910). *Diaries of Franz Kafka: 1910–1913*. Trans. Joseph Kresh. New York: Schocken, 1949.

Kafka, F. (1966). *Letter to His Father*. New York: Schocken.

Klein, M. (1930). The importance of symbol-formation in the development of the ego. *International Journal of Psychoanalysis*, 11: 24–39.

Lang, M. (2007). The hypochondriac: Bodies in protest from Herman Melville to Toni Morrison. Ph.D. Dissertation in Comparative Literature, Stony Brook University.

Levine, H.B. (2009). Time and timelessness: Inscription and representation. *Journal of the American Psychoanalytic Association*, 57: 333–355.

Lombardi, R. (2002). Primitive mental states and the body. *International Journal of Psychoanalysis*, 83: 363–381.

Lombardi, R. (2010). The body emerging from the "Neverland" of nothingness. *Psychoanalytic Quarterly*, 79: 879–909.

Lussheimer, P. (1954). On daydreams. *American Journal of Psychoanalysis*, 14: 83–92.

Marty, P. & De M'Uzan, M. (1963). La pensée opératoire [Mechanical functioning]. *Revue Française de Psychanalyse*, 27: 345–356.

Meltzer, D. (1964). The differentiation of somatic delusions from hypochondria. *International Journal of Psychoanalysis*, 45: 246–250.

Meltzer, D. (2009). *Dream-Life: A Re-Examination of the Psychoanalytic Theory and Technique*. London: Karnac.

Mitrani, J.L. (1995). Toward an understanding of unmentalized experience. *Psychoanalytic Quarterly*, 64: 68–112.

Mitrani, J. (2007). Some technical implications of Klein's concept of 'Premature Ego Development'. *International Journal of Psychoanalysis*, 88: 825–842.

Niederland, W.G. (1958). Early auditory experiences, beating fantasies and primal scene. *Psychoanalytic Study of the Child*, 13: 471–504.

Nissen, B. (2000). Hypochondria. *International Journal of Psychoanalysis*, 81: 651–666.

Rosenfeld, D. (1984). Hypochondrias, somatic delusion and body scheme in psychoanalytic practice. *International Journal of Psychoanalysis*, 65: 377–387.

Rosenfeld, H. (1958). Some observations on the psychopathology of hypochondriacal states. *International Journal of Psychoanalysis*, 39: 121–124.

Rosenfeld, H. (1964). On the psychopathology of narcissism: A clinical approach. *International Journal of Psychoanalysis*, 45: 332–337.

Rosenman, S. (1981). Hypochondriasis and invidiousness. *Journal of the American Academy of Psychoanalysis and Dynamic Psychiatry*, 9: 51–70.

Rosenman, S. & Handelsman, I. (1978). Narcissistic vulnerability, hypochondriacal rumination, and invidiousness. *American Journal of Psychoanalysis*, 38: 57–66.

Sandler, J. (1976). Countertransference and role-responsiveness. *International Review of Psychoanalysis*, 3: 43–47.

Schellekes, A. (2010). When time stood still: Thoughts regarding the dimension of time in primitive mental states. In Spero, M.H. (ed.), *Ma'arag –The Israel Annual of Psychoanalysis*, 1, pp. 281–303. Jerusalem: The Hebrew University Magnes Press, 2010.

Schellekes, A. (2017). When time stood still: Thoughts about time in primitive mental states. *British Journal of Psychotherapy*, 33(3): 328–345.

Sifneos, P.E. (1973). The prevalence of 'alexithymic' characteristics in psychosomatic patients. *Psychotherapy and Psychosomatics*, 22(2): 255–262.

Skogstad, W. (2013). Impervious and intrusive: The impenetrable object in transference and countertransference. *International Journal of Psychoanalysis*, 94: 221–238.

Spero, M.H. (1990). Portal aspects of memory overlay in psychoanalysis – An object relations contribution to screen memory phenomena. *Psychoanalytic Study of the Child*, 45: 79–103.

Starčević, V. (1989). Pathological fear of death, panic attacks, and hypochondriasis. *American Journal of Psychoanalysis*, 49: 347–361.

Steiner, J. (1993). *Psychic Retreats: Pathological Organizations in Psychotic, Neurotic and Borderline Patients*. The New Library of Psychoanalysis. London: Routledge,.

Stolorow, R.D. (1979). Defensive and arrested developmental aspects of death anxiety, hypochondriasis and depersonalization. *International Journal of Psychoanalysis*, 60: 201–213.

Sugarman, A. (2008). Fantasizing as process, not fantasy as content: The importance of mental organization. *Psychoanalytic Inquiry*, 28: 169–189.

Symington, N.(2014). Personal communication.

Tustin, F. (1981). *Autistic States in Children*. London: Tavistock/Routledge.

Tustin, F. (1990). *The Protective Shell in Children and Adults*. London: Karnac.

Valenstein, A.F. (1973). On attachment to painful feelings and the negative therapeutic reaction. *Psychoanalytic Study of the Child*, 28: 365–392.

Williams, G. (1997). Reflections on some dynamics of eating disorders: 'No entry' defences and foreign bodies. *International Journal of Psychoanalysis*, 78: 927–941.

Williams, P. (2004). Incorporation of an invasive object. *International Journal of Psychoanalysis*, 85: 1333–1348.

Winnicott, D.W. (1962). The theory of the parent-infant relationship – Further remarks. *International Journal of Psychoanalysis*, 43: 238–240.

Winnicott, D.W. (1971). *Playing and Reality*. London: Tavistock.

Chapter 6

Sentenced to life[1]

Reflections on trauma and the inability to bear vitality, following the movie *Turtles Can Fly*

In this chapter I invite you on a journey, not always an easy one, during which I contemplate conditions wherein the ability to experience vitality is damaged or non-existent, either as a result of a primary trauma or of a late-onset trauma. In such states, one is often faced with extreme internal turbulence that can be of such intensity as to endanger the very ability to sustain life. In short, using Beckett's succinct words: "You must go on, I can't go on, I'll go on" (Beckett 1953, p. 414).[2]

The main axis in this chapter will be the movie *Turtles Can Fly*, to and from which I will move while engaging in thoughts that are relevant theoretically and clinically when we work with patients who cannot bear their own vitality or that of others, so that an encounter between themselves and another person becomes a flooding, invasive emotional excess that is beyond one's ability to digest. This is a Kurdish feature film from 2004 that presents, with a moving and painful clarity, the complex fabric of relations between trauma and vitality.

From a broad professional perspective, it can be said that most people who seek psychotherapy/analysis have experienced a rupture in their ability to feel life in its fullness, to feel not merely that they are alive but that their life has been blessed by a good measure of creative forces and of vitality.[3] Put simply, one can say that vitality is disclosed through a person's ability to be active in their life in a manner that expresses their essence as a person, that enables them to experience a large gamut of affects and thoughts, to have interest in other persons and to be able to maintain emotional, meaningful and fertile contact with them.

Some time ago, a woman I shall call Amalia applied to me for therapy. Then in her fifties, she recounted how, despite success in many aspects of life, she felt herself to be empty, with no thoughts, no memories, because she "never visited there," thus expressing her inner disconnect from parts of herself in general, and from the realms of her childhood, in particular. Her first dream was about a recumbent woman who had eyes that could have been either eyes or camera shutters. Amalia approached the woman to peer into her eyes, since it was unclear whether the woman was Amalia herself or someone else, and whether she was alive or dead.

DOI: 10.4324/9781003479482-6

It was obvious to her that the dream was about feelings of life and death, but she emphasized that in her waking life she never "visited such questions," an interesting remark since her very reason to start therapy was related precisely to such questions. I said that, seemingly, when she dreamed, her eyes were able to look inwards into herself. Softly, Amalia added that, apparently, eyes were indeed the organ which admitted light in and which allowed something of the outside to enter while at the same time regulating just how much.

Gradually we talked about how she liked photographing reflections of light and how difficult it was for her to hold on to experiences and remember them, to the extent that she felt empty, though she obviously was not. Using the dream's images, it was unclear how wide her shutter could open to the outside world and let experiences in so that they could register and be remembered beyond the duration of their actual occurrence. She added that she liked to paint, that most of her paintings were formless and that occasionally another person would add figurative elements which gave the painting content and form, thus creating an experiential meaning that was previously lacking in her paintings.

I will not expand on the delicate and fascinating dialogue that emerged between us, since I am introducing this vignette here as a foil for clarifying and contrasting it with a different clinical state further on.

Amalia's state illustrates, in my view, an inner life capable of fantasizing and knowing fantasy from reality, of symbolization and self-reflection but which, despite its richness and creativity, remains inaccessible to the person herself and is experienced by her as an empty hole, without any awareness of the various mechanisms of disconnection, erasure and estrangement from her internal life. In Amalia's case, it gradually became clear to me that, from an early age, Amalia developed in a dual mental track. On one hand, due to a family context imbued with traumas that occurred prior to her birth, and to a significant measure of masked depression, which her parents hid behind a relatively invested functioning, she developed precocious mental abilities that became an envelope of intellectual brilliance very early on. In the extreme, this envelope acquired provocative and arrogant features, which gave her a feeling of excessive independence and omnipotence. On the other hand, an internal parallel track developed, in which the lack of object presence and of representations of such presence left her with an internal hole into which all her experiences sank, gradually disappearing. Thus, a significant part of her life occurrences was experienced but not represented, as if traceless, leaving her feeling as if she had no memories and no thoughts. It is therefore not surprising that, in spite of her abilities to function, Amalia needed at all times to adhesively, symbiotically and totally attach herself to a significant other's presence, whose emotional contour and internal representations became her own. This way she could stretch a covering net over the internal abyss and even be able to use her own creativity, but this thin net was soon prone to being ripped/torn, so that Amalia frequently fell into intense episodes of major depression, during which she felt a strong sense of emptiness and a lack of any vitality. In my view, a deep structural dissociation developed so that one part within her was alive and had various experiences, while another part did not register these experiences due to an inability to digest and represent them. This state echoes Botella and Botella's understanding of mental states in which the lack of representation is experienced as an excess of un-digestible stimuli that cannot be processed and thus becomes a traumatic experience (Green 1999; Botella & Botella 2005; Perelberg 2015). In such states, the part that is alive and vital becomes a threat to the part that cannot digest this vitality, to such an extent that many life events are not absorbed or are even erased. In other words, I am trying to describe a structure in which, although vitality exists and there is openness to new experiences, many of life's events are registered as a threatening and flooding excess, a sort of emotional tsunami (Bromberg 2008), by another part of the psyche. Consequently, one's experiences become shrunken or even evaporate because of the inability of this second part to regulate, digest and represent.[4] In such a state, it is not surprising that Amalia oscillated between aliveness and vitality (sometimes with hypomanic features), at one pole, and states of unbearable emptiness and deep depression, at the other pole.

In this dual-track structure, of vitality and its destruction, the clinical work is (relatively) more possible, since a terrible and continuous dread of contact with external reality as well as total shrinking from such contact have not developed. In contrast to Amalia's case, in many cases of massive trauma there is no such disconnect from oneself, but instead the individual lives feeling internally and externally overwhelmed, and utterly unable to curb this sense of inundation (Boulanger 2005). These are states lacking a clear distinction between inner and outer, between experience and fact, between the concrete and the symbolic, so that every painful internal event is perceived as if it were a real concrete happening, and every external event at once invades and colors the person's inner world. In such states, reality testing collapses, and one lives in a psychic-equivalence existence (Fonagy & Target 2002) in which thought and action become one; rigidity and concreteness replace symbolic thinking, and the differentiation between perception and interpretation or processing collapses too. One's encounter with one's alive parts, especially the painful ones, and one's contact with the outside world become a frightening and persecutory reality. Within such a reality, gradually every sign of aliveness and vitality, whether inside oneself or coming from outside, is experienced as an intolerable dread. Psychic energy is trapped in an inner flood which can be neither assimilated nor regulated. The person feels they have no choice but to gradually curtail any stimulus to feeling and all contact with the outside world, eventually leading a life of severely constricted scope and involvement.

In such cases, starting therapy or analysis arouses hope, but, simultaneously, anything that takes the patient closer to the possibility of encountering life feels paralyzingly threatening. One may say that such people are sentenced to life – that is, they are physically alive but without the tools to live life to the full. I will describe now some of the theoretical and clinical aspects of the existence led by people whom I have chosen to describe as *sentenced to life*.

First, I will illustrate some of the facets of the sentenced-to-life patient through my encounter with another patient, and later on through my discussion of the movie *Turtles Can Fly*.

Mona phoned me and in a feeble voice asked for a first meeting. The frailty and elusiveness of her weak voice had an immediate and powerful effect on me, forcing me to strain to catch her few barely audible words. We scheduled a session, but shortly before the time set she cancelled, as she felt unable to meet. Several weeks later, she phoned again, and we eventually managed to settle on a time to meet which she felt she could cope with. In the first session, she spoke in a frail voice, with many pauses, as if she were losing contact with both what she was saying and where she was, as if in a sort of fugue.

The account she gave of her life was elusive – on the one hand, a wonderful childhood, a warm and mutually devoted family but, at the same time, no unique special color attached to this family or to her within it. This emphasized the vagueness of this tissue of idealization, which created retrospectively an image of a wonderful and essentially different past, as compared to anything following the massive trauma she had endured. Everything was described as wonderful until adolescence, when she suffered serious physical injury accompanied by what she experienced as cold-heartedness in those responsible for the repeated occurrence of the traumas. All this left her feeling vulnerable and cut off, as if everything had come to a standstill (on time dimensions in trauma, see Terr 1984; Levine 2009b; Schellekes 2017), and years passed without her knowing how. Her life became steadily more constricted, but in a particular way: She could care for others with an exceptional sensitivity, creativity and instinctive understanding for nuances of emotion, but at the same time she had not the slightest volition or capacity to care for herself beyond the bare minimum necessary to get through life. Any encounter with people or obligations made her shrink back into herself and disconnect for days, alone at home, immersed in a state of bewilderment and unmooring.

Over a long interval, sessions with her were few, partial and far between. When we did meet, it seemed she had to make a great effort to arrive, and one session seemed to be enough for her for relatively long periods of time. In the sessions, I felt that any time I came verbally close, I was touching someone who had no skin at all, that she experienced everything with a terrible intensity, so threatening as to break her up (see 'thin skin syndrome' in Bick (1968), Rosenfeld (1987), Hopper (1991), Britton (1988)). Very soon I learned to choose my words very carefully and at the right temperature, so as not to frighten her off, since it seemed that any contact had to be limited to the amount she could bear or else she would experience a terrible catastrophe.

While any understanding of mine or emotional contact moved her, she at once also experienced it, I felt, as an inwash of life, which her psychic apparatus was incapable of absorbing. Any possibility of contact with the world frightened her badly, causing her to withdraw into a compulsive preoccupation with some trivial fact. Presented with the need to make a decision, she lapsed into paralysis, time passed, and the opportunity to intervene in her life passed by, and thus, time and again, Mona retreated into an isolated but safe existence. In the sessions, the discrepancy between her sensitivity and vitality towards other persons, as opposed to the impervious relation towards herself, was evident. This way, her life went on at a minimal level needed for survival.

I have concentrated on a few aspects of my sessions with Mona to stimulate our theoretical and clinical thinking when we are facing states in which a person lives life as though serving out some bitter and cruel sentence. In these extreme states, we are not witnessing a dual track of development and vitality, on one hand, and of dissociation and shrinking away, on the other hand, as I tried to describe in Amalia's case, but rather, we encounter states in which all switches have been turned off, such that any emotional experience will be disabled from creating a short circuit that will burn down the whole mental system. We can say that a permanent "smoke detector" (a concept introduced by van der Kolk (2002)) with many false alarms exists, since most of the events in present time echo past traumas and are experienced as identical with the most extreme internal dreads. Such a state can lead to extreme emotional opaqueness and avoidance, as a means of warding off the burst of an internal fire.

The therapeutic challenge of such states is enormous, since in the final analysis all therapies and analyses, and across all theoretical differences between analysts, bring the patient closer to their own life and to that of their significant others; or, more succinctly, try to help the patient lead a fuller life.

When the patient feels their life as a cruel decree, any therapeutic progress may evoke dread and be experienced as a toxic vitality. With Mona this issue was absolutely critical, since the degree of vitality and of connectedness to life, between her and herself and between her and me, had to be carefully measured – by both of us – lest there arose what I would term *toxemia of therapy*. This is a concept I propose for states in which the degree of distance between therapist/analyst and patient, the emotional temperature in interventions or within the session, the degree of the analyst's vitality, are all beyond the patient's ability to digest. Such a state might be experienced as a catastrophic flooding that threatens the very emotional existence of the patient. I have encountered such states several times with Mona. The most extreme one occurred in a session in which she surprisingly brought along a recording of music she had created in her youth, but not later, and asked me to listen to that music. She was intensely excited and asked not to be present in the room while I listened to the music. When she returned, I had tears in my eyes, deeply moved by the amazing voice and vitality that erupted from her songs and that stood in such deep contrast to Mona's emotional clogging and reduced life in the present. My tears were probably much beyond what Mona could bear, and she experienced them, in my understanding, as a fatal dose of intimacy and emotion. This generated long weeks of withdrawal and cancellation of sessions. I assume that my emotional reaction doubled her own, so that an internal hurricane developed not only in a quantitative sense but also as a mournful encounter with both her vitality and the loss of it. My tears thus rapidly became a very painful mirror of that internal encounter.

Notwithstanding a post-traumatic dimension being obvious in Mona's history, it also became clear that even before the traumatic occurrences the features I have described were present, if to a lesser degree, but had not brought about severe withdrawal. It seems that the late onset of the traumas severely broke Mona's thin defenses and left her dreading any encounter with her internal as well as external world. In these states, any vitality disappears to such an extent that any kind of contact is thoroughly avoided. This is not a case of double and parallel tracks, one of development and one of withdrawal and avoidance, as I described in Amalia's case, but a state of severe emotional blocking vis-à-vis any contact, since every contact is felt as burning and annihilating.

Before I move on to some theoretical and clinical dilemmas of this state, I would like to present some dimensions of the film *Turtles Can Fly*, as I feel they may provide a fascinating perspective of how its characters move complexly across the continuum between vitality $\longleftrightarrow$ aliveness $\longleftrightarrow$ (psychic) death.

In my view, this film unfolds, over and above its main social and political themes, a complex and moving human tapestry, showing that the spectrum between a vitality-filled life and a life experienced as a cruel decree is very wide indeed. The film is a 2004 Iranian-Iraqi co-production directed by Bahman Ghobadi, an Iranian of Kurdish descent, most of whose films deal with the hard fate of the Kurdish people, who, scattered over the borders between Iran, Iraq, Turkey and Syria, live without a state of their own. Most of Ghobadi's movies have been made outside Iran's borders, to ensure freedom of expression in general, and freedom to create in the Kurdish language, in particular.

The events of *Turtles Can Fly* occur just before the USA's invasion of Iraq in March, 2003, and the making of the film at this precise point in time fuses with the events it portrays. The film focuses on a group of Kurdish orphan children in a poverty-stricken village which has no running water, no electricity, no school, and sits on the frontier between Iraq and Turkey. All the characters are played by non-professionals recruited by Ghobadi from the very villages he portrays. The central character is known to everyone as 'Satellite' because of his skill at installing television satellite dishes. He is an artless yet charismatic 13-year-old orphan trickster, who leads and looks after a large posse of war orphans, who support themselves by dismantling, collecting, and selling the mines laid by Saddam Hussein's soldiers and by the American forces all over this border area. Some of the children have already lost limbs to their "trade." With the entry of the Americans into the region, the village elders are anxious to hear the television news as to when the attack on Iraq will begin, and so are dependent on Satellite for installing the necessary satellite dishes and for translating the broadcasts from English into Kurdish.

The landscapes against which the film takes place serve as more than background; they are a narrative device in their own right, as key as the screenplay itself: They are by turns arid and swampy, or else covered with snow, the latter symbolizing the purity of the Kurdish people, as Ghobadi disclosed in an interview (Kilic 2005). These landscapes are littered with ruins and dumps of wrecked weaponry and other junk,[5] which as well as forming the children's playgrounds constitute spaces that cry out their own terrible testimony.

Putting aside the socio-political backdrop, painful and fascinating as it is in itself, I would like to turn now to the film's human dimension, which sets out with remarkable sensitivity and anguish the dilemmas of life confronted by the refugee war orphans. Among these refugees are a 13- and 14-year-old brother and sister, Hengov and Agrin, and a much smaller blind child, Riga, who at first is presented as their little brother. All three have fled their own village after their parents' slaughter by Saddam's forces in the Halabja village massacre of the Kurds. The older brother, Hengov, lost his hands disarming mines but still earns his "living" in the same way, now using his mouth.

By and large, we may say that all of the children in the reality depicted in the film have been *sentenced to life* under the most extreme conditions, and have to fight even for that life. In my view, the fascination of the film is that it not only discusses the artificial political frontiers in which people are trapped but also the fine borders between being able to live – in the harshest of conditions – a life which has in it hope, fantasy, passion, creativity and vitality, as against sinking into a life experienced as an agonizing and hope-shattering life-sentence, in which the horror felt far outweighs any sign of vitality, leading inexorably to the choice of death as the sole imaginable place of peace.

Themes of life and death interweave from start to finish in the film, accentuating each other by force of contrast. For example, against a breathtaking landscape, the movie opens with a scene where a young girl stands on the edge of a precipice, pauses, and then jumps into the abyss, into the waters of the lake beneath. The girl's suicide lays down death as fact at the very outset, as though putting to death any hope the audience might have harbored. Then, immediately afterwards, the viewer meets Satellite, full of creativity, vitality and passion, a homeless orphan who recruits every part of his psyche to help him connect to life and to the hope invested in belonging to everything "American." He is a source of hope, leadership and parenting to everyone, deploying enormous charm and manipulativeness to "deliver the goods" – that is, the hope everybody stands in need of, and the love and respect he himself craves. For instance, he makes up the translation of the English news, although he hardly understands any English, and he pretends to negotiate deals with an American soldier, thus hoping for respect in the eyes of the orphans, when in reality the conversation is in Kurdish.

When he meets Agrin, he at once falls in love with her and tries to take her under his wing, and thus the fire of loving desire is intertwined into the girl's misery, for as the film unfolds, it is revealed that the small blind boy is not her little brother but the outcome of a vicious gang-rape by the Iraqi soldiers who stormed her village, killed her parents, and set the family's home on fire.

Agrin asks Satellite to get her a rope, which becomes the symbol of the bond between them as well as the rope which saves the little boy's life: His mother and uncle tether him with it so that he cannot wander off while they are at work disarming mines or while he is asleep (the boy is a somnambulist). By the end of the film, however, the same rope becomes an instrument of death.

Satellite is the herald of news and progress and, as such, the bearer of hope for renewal and liberation, even if these are figments of his creative imagination. He is a symbol of connectedness to life, of devotion and vitality, the enabler of cross-frontier and interpersonal communication – after all, he is a translator, even though the translation is wholly imaginary, as he knows no English.

His falling in love with the girl is also the fruit of the time-honored hope for "someone just like her" with whom to redefine lost family life. But the closer Satellite tries to get to the girl, to court her, to help her in various ways, the more she shrinks away from him as though overwhelmed by his vitality. For the greater part of the film the girl says nothing. The few sentences she does utter turn out later to have been attempts to get information about different ways of bringing about the end we know is coming.

Her little blind son is one of the most heart-rending figures in the whole film. It is as though his blindness stands for the necessity of not seeing all life's horrors, for, in such circumstances, to see things "straight" is to end any capacity for a life of vitality. The boy's blindness, I might say, also encapsulates his mother's desire – if only she could not see him there, alive, her child. She pleads with her brother, who cares for the little boy like a devoted parent, that the two of them should abandon him, as though putting physical distance between her and her son could work in reverse on the temporal level and erase the traumatic events of the past.

And, against her wish to walk away from him, the little boy is a permanent reminder of the atrocity of her traumas. Although her brother lives with the great pain of his sister's rape, of the loss of their parents, of his own crippling situation and the situation in general, despite everything, he manages to remain connected to life, to love his little nephew and care for him with remarkable gentleness, even as his sister persists in every possible way to try and rid herself of him.

The brother, seeing through the eyes of his spirit, has the gift of predicting the future, a *negative blindness*, I would say – a gift with manic qualities of omnipotence. There are moments when his foretelling ability furnishes the illusion of rescue from catastrophes, while at other moments the visions in his head confront him prematurely with disasters he is powerless to prevent. At such times, his omnipotent defenses are strengthened by his experiencing his prophetic vision as itself having brought about the disaster.

Riga, the little blind boy, traverses the whole gamut of emotion from naivety, playfulness and vitality to agony, misery and petrification. There are moments when he manages not to be aware of all the dimensions of the reality he lives in, when he retains innocence and hope and still calls his mother "Mommy" in spite of her refusal to identify with motherhood (even though in a few scenes an expression of tender worry for her son does wash over her face, an alive pain that her psyche is unable to contain). In one touching scene, the little boy, holding two turtles in his little hands, asks if they can be put into a pool to keep them alive, or perhaps, alluding to the film's title, to "let them fly."

At other moments, we see him sobbing next to barbed-wire fences or wandering around on his own among empty pipes, calling out "Daddy," as though in his isolation he is trying to connect to some parental presence via his pleading words to a father he has never known.

When all his girl-mother's entreaties to her brother fail to change the brother's mind, in an unusual storm of emotion she ties her son to a tree and leaves him there, in the hope that someone will find him and take care of him, or perhaps that he will tread on a mine. She moves away from him tearfully, as though seeing and hearing his pain and bewilderment is more than she can bear.

In a climactic scene, the village children approach Riga, who is still tethered to the tree. Although difficult to watch, the scene shows us again Satellite's determined hold on life, his readiness to put himself at risk for the sake of love, the village children's creative playfulness and little Riga's capacity to respond to all this, even for a few moments, with delight and vitality. Satellite tries to amuse the boy with a necklace of rifle cartridges (a very powerful image condensing eroticism, vitality and death), which he meant as a present for the boy's mother. Coming forward to pick up the necklace, the little blind boy is about to step on a mine. Satellite jumps in to save him.

Satellite does indeed save Riga's life but at the price of losing his own foot in the ensuing explosion. And, in fact, he has only saved the child for one further day of life, as the very next day his mother uses the rope Satellite gave her at the start of the film to tie him to a large rock and plunge him into the lake to drown. Thus, she erases both his existence and his right to life. It is a sort of symbolic equation, for she is attempting to concretely erase the traces of an unbearable trauma which is actually unerasable and which indeed has overwhelmed her psyche.[6] Here again the lake and its waters become a core multilayered theme of the film, for this is the very lake which it is claimed has beautiful red fish living in it, symbolic of life and eroticism, and which Satellite has been trying to catch to give to his beloved Agrin. When from this same lake another boy, the wounded Satellite's devoted admirer, brings him in excited pride the gift of several of the red fish, his joy at the sight of the fish rapidly turns into fright, as Satellite realizes that their red color is in fact blood pouring out of them. It was also into these very waters that little Riga had put the two turtles to let them swim back to life – that is, to fly. Thus, *Turtles Can Fly* is, in my view, a metaphor for one's efforts to lift off into the air (Schellekes 2019b), for manic defenses, for looking to connect to supernatural forces (such as the handless Hengov's foretellings), the forces without which it seems impossible to overcome such an intolerable internal and external reality. And finally, water is the element that receives little Riga's sinking body, drowned by his mother, and in which subsequently she herself finds her last rest – two turtles who will never again fly. Thus, the two images – of water and of turtles who can fly – are both molded by the film into an intermixing of life and death; after all, a flying turtle, one could say, is trying to go beyond its natural powers and, in so doing, endanger its life. Throughout the entire film, its characters are trying to navigate this intermingling of vitality and dead life, just as severely traumatized persons do, but in the end both Satellite and Agrin's brother are left with the terrible pain of loss. They are alive, but it is open to doubt whether there will be vitality in their lives or whether they will become a sort of satellite of planet Humankind, flying in its proximity but not really part of it.

Further thoughts in response to the film

When a child experiences at a very early age an emotional excess that is beyond its ability to digest, this excess becomes traumatic, whether as a result of a clearly traumatic event or as a result of a deep lack of a lively, regulating and transformational object representation. In such cases, a massive call is made on the psyche to erect defenses of all kinds against an in-flooding of traumatic stimuli which, in quantity and kind, are beyond the child's capacity to mentally represent and emotionally assimilate/digest (Botella & Botella 2005). The erection of these defenses frequently allows a dissociative re-organization which both protects against any encounter with traumatized parts of the personality and allows the parts unconnected to the trauma to develop relatively adequately[7] (Boulanger 2014; Gurevich 2014), as I have shown in Amalia's case.

To briefly return to Amalia, the first of my patients I cited at the beginning of this chapter, it is my opinion that a considerable part of her growing up was characterized by strong development along certain dimensions, which enabled living and creative parts of her to blossom. But simultaneously, primitive dissociative forces[8] were operating massively to make the events of her life pass without registering mentally over the long term. Her psychic shutter was tightly closed to the entry of the light and dark of reality, both internal and external. The events of her life continued to unfold, but she "never visited there." In this way, she lived a full life without most of its components receiving any acknowledgment or representation. In such a state, attacks of severe depression were to be expected, notwithstanding her considerable inner riches. Nor is it surprising that she came to therapy relatively late in life, for, as she saw things, therapy was liable to open her shutter more than she felt she could withstand. This is why her experience of her inner life oscillated between a sense of emptiness and a sense of a shadowy amorphous inner reality which while protecting her from live encounter with her inner world at the same time was a source of further distress, beyond her capacity to think or digest, except by acquiring form from external others (for instance, the other person who injected form into her paintings). And if we now return to Mona, the second patient mentioned, the trauma she suffered during adolescence occurred to a person with a very thin psychic skin, which, however, enabled her a relatively normal development until adolescence.[9]

The collision between the relatively late trauma and a fragile psychic structure overwhelmed her with severe physical sensations, confusion, anxiety and a sense of paralyzing helplessness. In my understanding, when trauma occurs at a more adult age, it does not allow the parallel/dual track of both stagnation and development, which often happens when the trauma occurs at a very early developmental stage, as in Amalia's case. At the later developmental age, lacking the capacity to compartmentalize the trauma and to protect itself from overwhelming inundation, the psyche shrinks and constricts more and more, loses its elasticity, collapses into rigidity, concreteness, dichotomized functioning and splitting off. In such circumstances, the constriction afflicts inner as much as outer, so that as contact with inner life diminishes, so does the ability to open up to live contact with the other or with reality. In the end, the person lives a life of deadness, waiting passively in some sort of motionless limbo.

During normal development (Bion 1970; Eigen 1996; Levine 2009a), progress and growth not only generate pleasure and satisfaction but also carry with them catastrophic anxiety at the prospect of change and descent into the unknown – which bears the awful potentiality of inner collapse. In this sense, change is also a developmental fracture. Gaddini (1982) deepens the understanding of this developmental paradox when he outlines two profound primary anxieties: One, anxiety of unintegration and fragmentation, and the other, no less powerful, anxiety of integration. As Gaddini sees it, any development in the direction of integration may be threatening, in that it constitutes one further step in the process of separation from the object and implies ego boundaries strong enough to permit the ego's existence apart from the object. When the process of self-formation has suffered severe disruption and been accompanied by severe separation anxiety, then any progress or development will always echo the loss-of-self anxiety and the anxiety of being left in a situation of overwhelming helplessness without the object. Integration anxiety thus frequently becomes a gatekeeper which, in therapy, ensures that progress is forestalled.

The more the psyche's resources are gathered to preserve a state of stasis – as happened with Mona – the more every movement in life, every interaction, fundamentally undermines the psyche and generates huge anxiety, as though another catastrophe has occurred. The only shield imaginable against this threat is stagnation, or as Mona put it, "I feel like sleeping for two months," for only when deeply asleep would she feel that life was not threatening to tear her apart. Further, this longing to stay in unchanging stasis embodies deep regressive yearnings, in that it enables an imaginary return to a profoundly infantile position, one which allows expression of frustrated infantile parts, if not through a sublimated and thoughtful expression, then through self-constriction, passivity and helplessness. If we consider the huge anxiety that seized hold of Mona when she applied to enter therapy, this step alone opened a crack in her wall of contraction and passivity. It was no surprise then that for many months her entry into therapy was beset, both actually and metaphorically, by waverings, disconnections, confusion, forgetfulness and dizziness, all of this requiring me to wage a sustained but delicately managed struggle to claim her back each time to a regular attendance, and to face up to live contact with herself and me.

This state of affairs recalls Grotstein's (2010) refreshing discussion on negative therapeutic reaction, in which he emphasizes that progress in therapy carries a threat to that primordial region of the psyche which still needs to shout out its neediness, through the fantasy of not growing up but remaining under a parental roof, whether real or imaginary. In Mona's case, her ability to care emotionally for helpless others offered her a sort of indirect self-therapy, for she plunged herself totally into their psyche, felt their feelings, identified with them, and so on the stage of her inner theater, she achieved vicarious fulfillment for her desire for absolute dependence. One can say that in her phantasy she became, at one and the same time, both patient and her own ideal therapist.

Let us return now to the girl Agrin, who effectively constitutes the central figure and ground for the whole movie and for this chapter. Her state and situation are those of unbearable cumulative trauma: She has been horribly raped at an age when her development was incomplete but, at the same time, too far advanced to allow her the option of compartmentalizing the traumatic event. To make things worse, the context of that trauma was a sequence of further severe traumas – her parents were murdered and she was made a refugee in losing her home. Her reaction to these overwhelming cumulative agonies is to constrict herself and to curtail almost all contact with the outside, for all the "outside" has lost any connotation of vitality. Instead, through a process of massive and concrete generalization, all "outside" has become equated with catastrophe. No wonder that the effect of Satellite's every vitality-full and desire-full move towards her drives her further into her shell of withdrawal. Thus, it is evident that Agrin's situation is much more entangled than Mona's or Amalia's because she does not have the option of disconnection. Her little son, helpless in his blindness, and absolutely dependent on her, is a constant reminder of her trauma and its consequences, not only the rape of her body but being raped into becoming a mother, before her time, before her psyche could recover from the preceding traumas. With Agrin, the blurring of the boundary between fantasy and reality, between attacker and victim, is more than the consequence of a past event: It is a continuing tragedy in her life, driving her to pursue the active re-enactment of the trauma and of her destruction (Hoffman 2003; Tutté 2004; Gerzi 2005; Gurevich 2014). Starting as a passive victim, she is driven to become the active executioner of her son and herself, in a sort of extreme identification with the aggressor (Ferenczi 1949; Howell 2014). This double murder becomes her one psychic rescue, in that it concretely erases what is psychically unerasable. Thus, the physical murder also becomes the murder of her thoughts and feelings, and, most importantly, the murder of her parenthood and her childhood, two dimensions which have been entirely extinguished in her psychic life and now, through death, also in physical reality.

In what might be a rush of optimism or of arrogance, I found myself wondering whether we as therapists/analysts could have saved Agrin had we met her. Would our analysts' credo have given us the capacity to act as the witness who validates her experience (Laub 1991; Caruth 1996; Amir 2017, 2018), who enables her to create a narrative of her trauma, transforming it into an event of the past rather than a continuous ever-present experience? Would the therapeutic relation have been able to create an encounter with her inner world in the presence of an attentive other who would assimilate for her what her own psyche could not (Boulanger 2005; Mészáros 2010)? Could a therapeutic/analytic process, conducted by the most talented therapist/analyst, have made it possible for her to bear a bearable amount of contact with a live person, which could have in turn enabled her to bear a bearable amount of vitality inside herself so that death would become an inner feeling rather than a concrete fact?

And, to go beyond Agrin, what about those other cases when our therapeutic power faces the challenge of being not only a potential for sustaining the patient's vitality but also the challenge that is provoking yearnings in the patient, yearnings whose fulfillment we cannot deliver and even risks being something too good/too alive for the patient to endure, thus contributing to the creation of the state I have named *toxemia of therapy*?

Many (Freud 1937; Bion 1965; Eigen 1996; Green 1999, 2001; Schellekes 2013, 2019a) have described mental situations which create an "aversion to life" (Ferenczi 1929) and a tendency of the psyche to assault and disintegrate itself in a process of hardening and self-emptying, driven by growth-resistant forces (Green 2001). This self-emptying guarantees the minimization of encounters with threatening parts of the psyche and of contact with the other. This happens particularly when the psyche is too frail to sustain its own vitality. These are states in which the central identification is with a state of non-being, and are the outcome of the absorption in early development of profound death anxieties which then took control over the psychic apparatus. In other words, when coming alive is simultaneously associated with re-traumatization, it is as if one is murdered every time one tries to come alive. As one comes alive, the object that murders life is intensely activated. As one puts oneself together, one also puts together the annihilating object (Eigen 2002). In such states, the boundary separating life from death loses cogency to the point that every move into the world of living experience is accompanied by a simultaneous threat of annihilation/cessation of existence. In other words, in this psychic state, to be born is to be murdered, so that the preferred solution is to remain psychically outside life in a state of stagnation and zero vitality (Gonzalez 2010; Modell 1999; Sekoff 1999).

I consider these to be extremely difficult dilemmas and, in my opinion, our professional discourse does not pay them sufficient attention. They are a part of our daily professional battle and of our suffering as therapists/analysts, for the encounter with these states is more than a theoretical dilemma, rather, in most instances, the painful intermingling of psyche in psyche, of trauma in trauma. This is an encounter which can drive us to escape the pain it entails by distancing ourselves or by clinging to the rescue fantasy[10] or, alternatively, by developing a position too vital for the capacity of the patient to bear, thus risking the emergence of what I formerly called *toxemia of therapy*.

I have tried to open up this complexity so that we can continue our search in perhaps less isolation, and so realize something of what Beckett (1953, p. 396) wrote elsewhere in his *The unnamable*, which I quoted from at the beginning of this chapter:

> Yes, in my life, since we must call it so, there were three things, the inability to speak, the inability to be silent, and solitude, that's what I've had to make the best of.

Notes

1 Schellekes, A. (2021). Sentenced to life – Reflections on the inability to bear vitality, following the movie *Turtles Can Fly*. In Prof. Dana Amir (ed.), *Ma'arag – The Israel Annual of Psychoanalysis, 9*, pp. 279–298. Jerusalem: The Hebrew University Magnes Press. The English version of this chapter is reproduced by permission of the *British Journal of Psychotherapy*, where it was published in a slightly different version: Schellekes, A. (2021). Sentenced to life: Reflections on the inability to bear vitality, following the movie *Turtles Can Fly*. *British Journal of Psychotherapy, 37*(3): 493–510. This article received the 2023 Hayman prize, given once every two years by The International Psychoanalytic Association for a published article pertaining to traumatized children and adults.

2 This paper was inspired by Frédérique Tecucianu and is dedicated to her memory. Frédérique was an Israeli and French clinical psychologist and close friend who passed away in 2014 in Paris, when she could no longer stand the battle with her terminal illness. Until her last living moments, her vitality and love of life

constituted a major source of support and inspiration for me, and echoes of her presence enlarged the space of my thinking in writing this chapter. Thus, only through an observing stance that combines a movement between memory, vitality and life, and between the loss of all these, can one speak about the essence of vitality.

3 The theoretical meaning of "vitality" will shift in accordance with the theoretical "roof" under which the discussion takes place. To illustrate, if somewhat schematically, in Bionian thinking vitality will be the outcome of the ability to move freely to and fro between the schizo-paranoid position and the depressive position; the ability to digest emotion and render it meaningful and, no less, the ability to experience while lacking knowledge or understanding. In Winnicottian terms, the emphasis in defining vitality would be on the individual's ability to express the 'true' kernel/core of his/her personality, since only contact with that kernel gives us the degree of creativity required for a living connectedness to life. It is this linkage, Winnicott would say, which makes possible the creative dance of motility between connection to reality and illusion, a creativity without which it is hard to feel any vitality. Over and above the particular emphases in the definition of vitality imposed by any theory, there are of course shared elements, a key one being our ability to exist psychically in the absence of the object and, equally key, our ability to maintain the connection to the object, without the ego feeling that that connection threatens its existence.

4 In this context, it is relevant to mention Fairbairn's concept of "anti-libidinal ego" (Fairbairn 1954, 1994) – that part which functions as an internal saboteur attacking the alive and vital part.

5 In this context, Trigg (2009) has an interesting perspective on the historical, emotional and geographical significance of ruins and wrecks. As he sees it, they site the memory of a trauma which remains affectively and historically connected to the site where the trauma occurred. The wreckage provides an alternative narrative in which evidence of the trauma is furnished by emptiness and absence rather than by presence.

6 Boulanger's view is pertinent here (Boulanger 2005), that massively traumatized persons lose the ability to tell external from internal, so that the external world turns into a direct mirror of their worst thoughts, fantasies and nightmares.

7 With early trauma, another important curative resource is the child's significant adults, as long as they validate the very occurrence of the trauma and help the child render it meaningful and process it, so as to make it digestible in terms of the child's developmental capacity. In all these ways, adults can act to reduce the level of disassociation, which otherwise will devour so much psychic strength; adults can enable the child's psyche to work through what has happened, so vital in preventing the trauma from being compartmentalized within the psyche, or alternatively massively flooding it. Unfortunately, there are many instances of "double" trauma, of "absence within absence" (Gurevich 2014), when to the first trauma is added a second, when parental figures fail to acknowledge the trauma and so fail to offer themselves as absorbers and regulators of the child's traumatic experience.

8 In this context, it is important to remember that the action of massive dissociation is not a passive and quiet process in which parts of the ego separate from each other but, on the contrary, a process of concealed aggression in which one part of the psyche attacks other parts, reducing them to a severely constricted state. Kalsched (2003) describes how in various traumatic states an all-powerful psychic apparatus emerges which tries to block the entry into consciousness of any painful or fragile emotional element. Any emergence of emotion or any attempt to approach the other is experienced as bearing the potential for "re-traumatization," so that the inner "Satan" at once attacks these ego parts and thereby attacks and eliminates any possibility of change or hope.

9 One can assume that Mona's idealizing tendency covered and concealed an early unrepresented lack or absence of a primary object, but there was not enough proof to validate this assumption.

10 See in this context Berman's discussion on rescue fantasies in countertransference (Berman 1997).

References

Amir, D. (2017). Traumatic miss and the work of mourning. *Fort Da*, 23(2): 7–16.

Amir, D. (2018). Awakening to and from the Traumatic Lacuna. *Psychoanalytic Quarterly*, 87: 303–321.

Beckett, S. (1953). The unnamable. In *Three Novels*. New York: Grove Press, 1958.

Berman, E. (1997). Hitchcock's vertigo: The collapse of a rescue fantasy. *International Journal of Psychoanalysis*, 78: 975–988.

Bick, E. (1968). The experience of the skin in early object-relations. *International Journal of Psychoanalysis*, 49: 484–486.

Bion, W.R. (1965). *Transformations: Change from Learning to Growth*. London: Tavistock.

Bion, W.R. (1970). *Attention and Interpretation*. London: Tavistock.

Botella, C. & Botella, S. (2005). *The Work of Psychic Figurability: Mental States Without Representation*. Hove and New York: Brunner-Routledge.

Boulanger, G. (2005). From voyeur to witness: Recapturing symbolic function after massive psychic trauma. *Psychoanalytic Psychology*, 22(1): 21–31.

Boulanger, G. (2014). *A model for understanding and treating adult onset trauma*. Lecture given at The Israel Psychoanalytic Society.

Britton, R. (1998). *Belief and Imagination: Explorations in Psychoanalysis*. New York: Routledge.

Bromberg, P.M. (2008). Shrinking the tsunami: Affect regulation, dissociation, and the shadow of the flood. *Contemporary Psychoanalysis*, 44(3): 329–350.

Caruth, C. (1996). *Unclaimed Experience: Trauma, Narrative and History*. Baltimore, MD: Johns Hopkins University Press.

Eigen, M. (1996). *Psychic Deadness*. London: Karnac.

Eigen, M. (2002). A basic rhythm. *Psychoanalytic Review*, 89(5): 721–740.

Fairbairn, R. (1954). *An Object-Relations Theory of the Personality*. New York: Basic Books.

Fairbairn, R. (1994). Endopsychic structure considered in terms of object relation-ships. In *Psychoanalytic Studies of the Personality*. London: Tavistock Publications with Routledge & Kegan Paul. (Original work published 1952).

Ferenczi, S. (1929). The unwelcome child and his death-instinct. *International Journal of Psychoanalysis*, 10: 125–129.

Ferenczi, S. (1949). Confusion of the tongues between the adults and the child – (The language of tenderness and of passion). *International Journal of Psychoanalysis*, 30: 225–230.

Fonagy, P. & Target, M. (2002). Early intervention and the development of self-regulation. *Psychoanalytic Inquiry*, 22(3): 307–335.

Freud, S. (1937). Analysis terminable and interminable. *International Journal of Psychoanalysis*, 18: 373–405.

Gaddini, E. (1982). Early defensive fantasies and the psychoanalytical process. *International Journal of Psychoanalysis*, 63: 379–388.

Gerzi, S. (2005). Trauma, narcissism and the two attractors in trauma. *International Journal of Psychoanalysis*, 86(4): 1033–1050.

Gonzalez, F. (2010). Nothing comes from nothing: Failed births, dead babies. In van Buren, J. and Ashanti, S. (eds), *Primitive Mental States – A Psychoanalytic Exploration of the Origins of Meaning*. New York: Routledge.

Green, A. (1999). *The Work of the Negative*. London: Free Association Books.

Green, A. (2001). *Life Narcissism, Death Narcissism*. London and New York: Free Association Books.

Gorstein, J.S. (2010). "Orphans of O": The negative therapeutic reaction and the longing for the childhood that never was. In van Buren, J. and Alhanati, S. (eds), *Primitive Mental States: A Psychoanalytic Exploration of the Origins of Meaning*. New York: Routledge.

Gurevich, H. (2014). The return of dissociation as absence within absence. *American Journal of Psychoanalysis*, 74(4): 313–321.

Hoffman, L. (2003). Vicissitudes of aggression: Theoretical and technical approaches to psychic trauma. *Journal of the American Psychoanalytic Association*, 51(2): 375–380.

Hopper, E. (1991). Encapsulation as a defense against the fear of annihilation. *International Journal of Psychoanalysis*, 72: 607–624.

Howell, E.F. (2014). Ferenczi's concept of identification with the aggressor: Understanding dissociative structure with interacting victim and abuser self-states. *American Journal of Psychoanalysis*, 74(1): 48–59.

Kalsched, D.E. (2003). Daimonic elements in early trauma. *Journal of Analytical Psychology*, 48(2): 145–169.

Kilic, D. (2005). *The Representation of Kurdish Identity and Culture in the Films of Bahman Ghobadi*. Kurdishmedia.com

Laub, D. (1991). Truth and testimony – The process and the struggle. *American Imago*, 48(1): 75–91.

Levine, H.B. (2009a). Reflections on catastrophic change. *International Forum of Psychoanalysis*, 18(2): 77–81.

Levine, H.B. (2009b). Time and timelessness: Inscription and representation. *Journal of the American Psychoanalytic Association*, 57(2): 333–355.

Mészáros, J. (2010). Building blocks toward contemporary trauma theory: Ferenczi's paradigm shift. *American Journal of Psychoanalysis*, 70(4). 328–340.

Modell, A.H. (1999). The dead mother syndrome and the reconstruction of trauma. In Kohon, G. (ed.), *The Dead Mother – The Work of André Green*. London: Routledge.

Perelberg, R.J. (2015). On excess, trauma and helplessness: Repetitions and transformations. *International Journal of Psychoanalysis*, 96(6): 1453–1476.

Rosenfeld, H.A. (1987). *Impasse and Interpretation*. London: Routledge.

Schellekes, A. (2013). Arid mental landscapes and avid cravings for human contact-Beckettian and analytic narratives. *EPF Bulletin*, 2013.

Schellekes, A. (2017). When time stood still-thoughts about time in primitive mental states. *British Journal of Psychotherapy*, 33(3): 328–345.

Schellekes, A. (2019a). Arid mental landscapes and avid cravings for human contact –Beckettian and analytic narratives. *British Journal of Psychotherapy*, 35(1): 91–106.

Schellekes, A. (2019b). The dread of falling and dissolving – Further thoughts. *British Journal of Psychotherapy*, 35(3): 448–467.

Sekoff, J. (1999). The undead: Necromancy and the inner world. In Kohon, G. (ed.), *The Dead Mother – The Work of Andre Green*. The New Library of Psychoanalysis. London and New York: Routledge.

Terr, L.C. (1984). Time and trauma. *Psychoanalytic Study of the Child*, 39: 633–665.

Trigg, D. (2009). The place of trauma: Memory, hauntings, and the temporality of ruins. *Memory Studies*, 2: 87–101.

Tutté, J.C. (2004). The concept of psychical trauma: A bridge in interdisciplinary space. *International Journal of Psychoanalysis*, 85(4): 897–921.

van der Kolk, B.A. (2002). Posttraumatic therapy in the age of neuroscience. *Psychoanalytic Dialogues*, 12(3): 381–392.

Chapter 7

Stations along the Via Dolorosa of good enough endings[1]

In what follows, I present certain reflections concerning the wish, which many of us share, to attain a good-enough ending of analysis. In my view, this wish raises many questions about the essential nature of the analysis that accomplishes a good ending and about the many analyses or therapies in which the process of reaching this yearned-for – and often illusory – position is a protracted path of torment and painful contractions, sometimes for both parties involved. As I contemplated these questions, Nathan, a delicate man who was my patient, came to mind. Nathan first came to see me in distress related to moving into a new job position within the highly demanding and esteemed medical field in which he already successfully practiced. Nathan was a sensitive and wise person, with kind, innocent eyes, a propensity for giving to others, a family he dearly loved and a subtle, self-deprecating sense of humor. All these qualities were interwoven with a thin yet prominent thread of anxiety about failure, and about difficult transitions between demanding job positions, invariably experienced by him as searing defeats. The very possibility of these failures flooded his mind with mild yet persistent waves of anxiety, which he tried to ward off with his intellectual capacities and obsessive defenses. Still, each new opportunity left him feeling terrified and unsafe, despite his numerous strengths and the considerable support he received from the people around him. In these painful situations, what stood out was how difficult it was for Nathan to bear psychic pain.[2] This difficulty created yet another layer of anxiety, pressing Nathan to come up with immediate solutions to any psychic challenge that arose.

I saw Nathan for about a year. He attended our sessions very regularly and, meticulous as he was, went to great lengths to share any material which he felt might be relevant to our work. We established a good, pleasant and tender therapeutic relationship, in which Nathan's considerable and compulsive repetitiveness concerning various topics was also evident. He seemed to be going around and around in a closed loop that seemed to guarantee the compartmentalization of any emotional complexity and the minimization of encounters with anything that might have surprised him or made him feel less in control. Nathan's condition gradually subsided and, at the time, I felt that

DOI: 10.4324/9781003479482-7

as the anxiety surrounding his professional position – with which he was constantly preoccupied – diminished we would be able to reach and deepen the contact with the other layers of his psyche. Those layers, in my view, led to the kind of emotional functioning that, while pleasant and safe, lacked depth and breadth, and was very limited in coping with emotional complexities beyond a certain level.

In this period of respite, Nathan felt that the therapy had helped him significantly, that he was capably handling his new position at work (which he had dreaded so much), that we had touched on highly meaningful material, and that he was ripe and ready to end. In his view, it had been a good and successful therapy. On my part, I found myself getting into an elaborate discussion with myself – and partially with Nathan – about his choice to terminate, feeling a big gap between his experience of having had a good therapy and my experience that it would be right to continue. Given how things had stabilized for him, I imagined that we would now be able to dwell in those areas of his psyche that needed more time, a slower pace, an encounter with states of not-knowing, with harsh self-demands and with more regressive needs. Most of all, I felt this was an opportunity for a less guarded encounter than had previously been possible with the ghosts of his past, a past which he often depicted in an idyllic and nostalgic manner. In contrast with my reflections, Nathan saw no need to continue the process. I told myself that I should accept his choice, that for him this was a good-enough therapy and that he felt no need to explore his psyche more deeply – as my perspective, perhaps, compelled me to expect. I also hoped that the therapeutic process would not end with the formal termination but would continue to unfold in Nathan's psyche, without my concrete presence, as often happens after endings.

Several years later, Nathan came back to see me in a similar predicament: Once again it concerned a role change at his work, with similar anxieties. This time, however, the intensity of his anxiety was far more acute, to the extent that he needed anti-anxiety medication. For a certain time, the therapy mainly focused on the pain involving the recognition that Nathan might stumble while climbing the ladder of excellence and perfection that he saw as his rightful trajectory. This ladder was a key life-organizing axis for him: Deep within his psyche, Nathan held on to a rich image of a wonderful, successful life, of a happy childhood for which he longed as a place he envisioned as peaceful and carefree (though this notion of the past, in my view, was considerably contaminated by the obfuscation and simplification so typical of the texture of nostalgia and idealization). Within this idyllic worldview, Nathan was used to positioning himself and his worth on a high rung, where perfection and success were axiomatic. Any slight undermining of these sent waves of anxiety – some apparent and some unseen – flooding through Nathan, since upholding a functioning façade was a key goal and an achievement in and of itself.

Much like the first stretch of therapy, this time it also felt as if Nathan's mind was burdened by psychic and interpersonal complexities, both past and present, that he felt forced to confront. Once again, as his symptoms subsided, he decided to terminate this phase of the therapy as well, after a relatively short time, proceeding with just the medication. Yet again, I was left with the need to do extensive internal work in order to accept the fact of this termination, despite not feeling that it was good-enough. In fact, I was left to deal with what Nathan himself found difficult to face; namely, the gap between his experience and what I sensed was necessary – a more comprehensive therapy that would deepen and broaden not only Nathan's ability to withstand being potentially disappointed with himself but also his capacity to lead a psychic life that contained a greater range of experience, where threatening primary deprivations, derivatives of aggression, emotional complexities and psychic pain were expressed and given room to be. Once again, I felt that termination at this point was deemed good-enough by Nathan while my own thoughts about continuing the therapy indicated my different perspective – which may have been correct or may have been tinged with ambition. Mainly, my thoughts about continuing the therapy were distressing for Nathan. Thus, with much warmth and with Nathan's significant gratitude for this 'good-enough' ending, we parted ways. Some eighteen months later, in one of my meetings with Nathan's psychiatrist, who is a dear and esteemed friend of mine, he asked me if I had heard that, several days earlier, Nathan had hung himself, thereby joining the little cemetery that the psychiatrist was carrying with him in his mind.

Dumbfounded and overwhelmed by sadness, I realized that yet another, more difficult challenge that Nathan found himself facing at that time, with its potential to create anxiety and uncertainty, proved beyond his 'good-enough' capacities to contain and metabolize and, to everyone's astonishment, he chose to end his life. A kind and honest man who gave so much to those around him, whose psychic capacities proved too constrained for life's complexity. Through his death, he created an ending more dramatic than any self-expression he allowed himself in life; an ending difficult enough to make its echoes reverberate and sink in deeply in all of us, all those whose lives had ever touched this good-enough man, who was too good and too frightened to live a life that he might have experienced as not good-enough. It is in his memory that I write this chapter.

It is indeed possible, at this point, to delve far more deeply into Nathan's psychic material, to analyze the course of his therapy and his decision to end the suffering of his not-at-all-bad life. For now, however, I choose to place Nathan as a kind of backdrop to my reflections, a screen on which I will project some thoughts about what contributes to endings that are not good-enough – which are far more numerous than what is usually reported through the illusory model of linear-development characteristic of so many case presentations, as manifest through expressions such as "from hell to heaven," "from the black hole to psychic birth," etc.

The thoughts I would like to dwell on have to do with what often appears, whether directly or indirectly, as qualities, obstacles, dead ends or terrors within the patient, the analyst and the space between them, which render many an ending far from good enough, by any criterion we may choose.[3] The analogy to the stations on Via Dolorosa that Jesus went through is meant to emphasize here the long, intricate and, at times, tormented process that both analyst and analysand go through. This process is not a singular or linear path, as we might say Jesus' was, but the various "stations" that I suggest describe specific challenges, complications and lacunae that exist in the analyst–analysand interaction, that may have a great impact on the quality of the process and its ending. These "stations" may intercalate with and augment each other, thus creating the complexities I try to describe. In the following discussion, I will limit myself to a small number of reflections from my broader preoccupation with this issue and from the various possible perspectives on it.

First station: Losing the distinction between resemblance and identicalness

In many long-term therapies and analyses – which tend to entail a powerful transference, significant psychic work and a close and deep emotional bond between the two parties – as the therapy or analysis progresses, the yearning and need felt by the patient for the analyst sometimes grow more potent. The patient, who experiences the analyst as a figure possessing essential and meaningful parental qualities, sometimes reaches extreme states in which it might prove difficult to maintain the distinction between the analyst as *resembling* a parental figure and as an *actual* parent. The patient's experience might reach a point where the analyst is felt to be an actual parent, whether through immersion in very intense regression, whether through the collapse of the distinction between the concrete and the symbolic, or whether through internal and external forces that exert a powerful pull on the analyst. The latter, in turn, might find themselves impelled – either knowingly or through internal blindness – to inhabit an emotional position which diminishes and even outright effaces the distinction between their parental role and becoming an actual parent, as in cases of transference psychosis. In all these states, one sometimes reaches extreme situations in which the ability to experience the setting, limited as it may be, as beneficent and protective, as a space that recalls and symbolizes parental holding – but not actual parenting – collapses alongside the growing expectation that all limitations – of time, space and the nature of the relationship – should disappear, and alongside the growing pressure to enable the concrete and total devotion of an actual parent to the youngest of infants.

This is often manifest in statements such as, "If you care about me, why do I need to pay?" or else, "Why do I have to come *here*,whereas you won't come to my house?" The more primary the mental state, the more these situations tend to arise. I do not view these situations as manipulative attempts to cause the analyst to "transgress" their boundaries and to collapse as a reliable parent but as the expression of primary yearnings. In these situations, considerable osmotic pressure is applied to turn patient and analyst into a single unit which thinks and feels in an identical and uniform manner. Quite often, the analyst's ability to transgress the limits of their capacities is an important one, facilitating the experience of unity that the patient needs at certain points in analysis. However, these situations often give rise to a pervasive difficulty in containing mistakes, imperfections, misunderstandings, less-than-complete overlap of emotional mood, the analyst's looking away, etc. Any incongruity evokes in the patient an experience of deep pain, of disappointment so bitter that it is catastrophic. To the extent that these are experienced by a psychic infrastructure that is unable to absorb imperfection, partiality and separateness, they might lead to premature termination, involving a painful experience of abandonment or extreme hurt.

In this context, Gaddini's thinking (1982) suggests that, insofar as the primary experiences of separateness between self and object have been experienced as traumatic, there is a greater risk that any developmental stage that requires one to move towards separateness and independence will resonate the catastrophic terror that accompanied the emergence of one's initial awareness of separateness in early development, which left the baby feeling intolerably small, vulnerable and fragile. In these situations, when any developmental movement towards separateness arouses terror, any change might be experienced as a threat to one's very existence, giving rise to a dismantling anxiety that Gaddini termed "integration anxiety" (1976, 1982). In this situation, there is a greater chance of seeing the formation of rigid defenses against any change whatsoever, of pervasive passivity, of clinging to a dependent and difference-effacing position and, in more extreme instances, of even favoring self-controlled fragmentary states, which are experienced as a lesser (and less frightening) evil, compared to states of integration and development, since the former are partially familiar to the person through the unintegrated states experienced in early development. These dynamics might lead to a "one-step-forwards, two-steps-backwards" scenario, which will maintain the balance that keeps the patient in a position of massive dependence. This trend thus often leads to an inability to experience an ending as psychically possible.

Another variation of the same difficulty in tolerating the complexity of similarity between the analytic situation and certain life experience situations lies in a powerful love transference. In such an intense transference, there is a growing blurring of distinction between the real and deep emotion developed towards the analyst in the analytic situation and a feeling of love towards, or being enamored of, someone outside the analysis. In the cases I am referring to, the analyst may become imbued/flooded with considerable intensities of love expressed towards him by the patient, which are, in fact, directed towards a different, past or present, figure in the patient's life.[4] Many times it becomes very difficult to refrain from experiencing the analysis as a real relation and from actualizing it as if it were identical to a romantic one. Sometimes, the blurring of this distinction between transference love and love outside the transference is yet another iteration of the difficulty depicted above, concerning the distinction between a parental therapeutic figure and an actual parent, except that now this difficulty is covered by a veil of sexual maturity. Quite often, the combination of intense primary needs and intense, more mature, sexual needs creates a boiling erotic lava in the transference. This poses a unique challenge to the analytic process, as the sheer force of this lava presses towards enactment and against analytic reflection. Such intense transference love is, naturally, multi-faceted in terms of the foundations governing its emergence, but the aspect I wish to emphasize here is the massive emotional pressure applied to both parties, a pressure which, barring good-enough working-through within the analysis, might accelerate termination. Some of these terminations occur when the analytic envelope has ruptured and can no longer facilitate the essence of the analytic work. Sometimes, such terminations will have the semblance of a good-enough ending while hiding the emotional turmoil teeming in the psyche of one – or sometimes both – of the people involved.

Second station: Emptying out defenses, toxemia of therapy

There are many situations in which there is overwhelming psychic pain that is greater than the psyche's ability to contain, whether due to severe holes in early development foundations or to elements of later severe trauma. In Nathan's case, one might say that his self-containment capacities were quite limited and drew chiefly on an excessive use of rationality. This meant that any situation that challenged the experience of perfection he so craved felt catastrophic. In many states when the psyche feels overwhelmed by excessive stimuli that surpass its containment capacities, we witness a process in which the psyche increasingly attacks itself, straining to sever the cord of experience and empty itself, to the extent of self-annihilation. This is done as an implicit, often unconscious attempt to reduce the amount of un-metabolizable internal and external stimuli (Schellekes 2021a, 2021b).

These are very difficult states in which the psyche attacks all linking – between different parts of the self, between self and other, between elements of thinking – gradually leading to the impoverishment of thought and emotion, even to the extent of reaching severe white psychosis (Donnet & Green 1973), as depicted by Bion (1959) and, following him, Grotstein (1990), or physical deterioration into a state of illness, as aptly described by French analysts Green (2005), Marty (1968), Aisenstein and Smadja (2010), and Miller (2014). These self-emptying states are particularly difficult in analysis or therapy, as the patient, while physically present, might be increasingly psychically absent, consumed by the voided-out state created by their psyche

(Schellekes 2019a). Voiding safeguards one from the pain one would have experienced had one's psyche remained overwhelmed with the explosive psychic materials it experienced, whether due to an insufficiently stable mental foundation, to traumatic elements that attack and overwhelm the psyche, or to a psychic structure saturated by the death drive. Despite the self-emptying efforts, these extreme psychic situations might result in states of intolerable excess that are evoked by any emotional stimuli, including the mere presence of the analyst. At times, this may give rise to what I have termed "toxemia of therapy" (Schellekes 2021a, 2021b) – a condition in which the analyst's presence or any interaction with them (including the various elements of such interaction) are experienced as an excessively overwhelming attack in relation to the absorption capacities of the psyche, which strains to empty itself of its vitality and of any trace of emotional stimuli. In this state, any emotional contact, even ostensibly pleasant or positive, might short-circuit the psychic system and be experienced as a threat to the patient's very emotional existence.

In such states of massive defensive self-emptying, the analyst may become a receptacle of vitality, while the patient is thrust from their own interiority to live a life of void, emptiness, failure and suffering. This may be compounded by insufficiently worked through salvation wishes on the part of the analyst, wishes that are often experienced by the patient, whether directly or indirectly, as an excessive and overwhelming dose of vitality which exacerbates the un-metabolizable gap that already exists in the patient's psyche between the yearning for vitality and the compulsion to deaden it. In such moments in therapy, once toxemia of therapy has set in, there is little chance for a good-enough ending: Sooner or later, the patient is liable to feel that they can no longer inhabit the therapeutic space and the encounter with the analyst, regardless of how aware they are of this complexity. In other words, one might see the emergence of two parallel tracks that are painfully and frustratingly discrete – one that expresses the *progressive* tendencies that the analysis/analyst seeks to facilitate eventually (though this may require considerably regressive periods); and one that expresses the patient's *voiding and links-attacking* tendencies. These are like two trains running on parallel tracks in opposite directions, although they seemingly aspire to reach the same desired destination.

In this connection, something less often addressed in our professional discourse is the opposite version of these two parallel trains going in different directions: The one where the *patient* is in a progressive state, with a true capacity for movement and development, while the *analyst*, tainted by a streak of personal and professional masochism, pulls downwards and favors dwelling on layers of pain and fragmentation, which they experience as the ultimate platform for profound analytic work. In my view, this state of affairs often slips under the radar of our professional consciousness, leading to various situations in which the analyst finds it difficult to relate to the patient's inklings of change and vitality and to support their emergence out of a misguided fear of neglecting those wounded parts of the psyche on which their therapeutic lens has grown accustomed to focusing – and even become fascinated with. (I elaborate on this in my fourth reflection below.)

Third station: Overloading of the analyst's psyche

We may also encounter the opposite variation of being emotionally overwhelmed, in those situations where the patient, instead of emptying their psyche, must face being deluged without any defenses and without active means of psychic emptying out. In such instances, the extent of the influx is so great that the patient will need the analyst's psyche as a place into which they can massively externalize and "vomit" psychic material, far beyond the analyst's ability to contain. Today, as we are increasingly aware of the primary needs of many of our patients, our clinical considerations allow us to be more flexible about the setting, to allow various modes of correspondence between sessions, for instance. Such accommodations allow the patient to feel that their overflooded psyche is undergoing a kind of "dialysis" by means of the analyst's psyche, a detoxification process that is often mind-saving and even life-saving. Nevertheless, in extreme situations, one might encounter the kind of "toxemia of therapy" in which, after a certain point, the *analyst's* psyche becomes so extensively and intensively overwhelmed that their own "dialysis machine" is attacked and even taken out of commission. Sometimes, massive pressure (which is often unconscious and unformulated) is put on the analyst to actually become the bad, sadistic, perverse, impervious or abandoning object the patient has experienced in the past. By becoming this object, the analyst is allowing the patient, to a certain extent and for a certain time, to engage in renewed dialogue and interaction with the primary object, though in a relatively sheltered therapeutic space. This may even liberate the patient from the presence of this difficult object, by virtue of its externalization and temporary insertion into the analyst. However, this potential, even beneficial, therapeutic path (whether we formulate it in Kleinian, Winnicottian or intersubjective terms, with all the essential and semantic differences between these approaches) does not unfold in all therapies. Often, the analyst struggles against or is too threatened by the forcefulness of the pressure applied to them to become the massive bad object, in its various manifestations, especially if it involves an object-quality from which their own psyche is trying to free itself. In such situations, therapeutic tragedies might ensue, leaving both parties afflicted by the same severe "toxemia of therapy," which overloads their psychic containment capacities. Now, one of the dangers facing the analyst is that they might try to free themselves of their role prematurely, as a way of ridding themselves of the pressure to become the bad object – the same object the analyst is internally struggling with anyway, either wittingly or unwittingly. Apparently, the experienced and conscious-enough analyst is indeed aware of this internal struggle, but the terror of being drawn by the bad object, which never completely ceases to exist in their psyche, might lead them to premature termination, before the patient has had the opportunity to complete their analyst-assisted psychic dialysis, which requires long stretches of time, sometimes proving too long for the analyst's psychic stamina.

Fourth station: Analyst's mistaken understanding of the patient's dominant level of psychic organization

Another station I wish to mention on the Via Dolorosa towards the longed-for good-enough ending is the analyst's confusion or blindness about the patient's level of psychic organization, meaning that the level of the former's interventions, their manner of listening and the quality of their interpretations might fail to correspond to the latter's level of development. Usually, only one direction of this gap is addressed when depicting the analyst's ostensible overestimation of the patient, meaning that the analyst works with the patient as if the latter operates in a more developed register, when this is often not the case. Our knowledge of and understanding about the various qualities of primitive mental states allow us to attune our analytic listening, the qualities of our interventions and the analytic process as a whole, including its ending, to the primary developmental layer the patient inhabits. Thus, for example, the analyst's level of emotional/mental/sensorial internal activity may increase, as they are often required to spread out a safety/holding net that is dense enough to keep the parts of the patient's psyche from leaking through its holes and through those of the overly perforated net of the patient's own psyche. The density of the analysis' holding net is manifest in the nature of the setting, the frequency of the sessions, the extent to which the analyst uses themselves – their own thoughts, the visual and auditory images that arise in them during analysis (see Botella and Botella's (2005) notion of figurability), their own physical sensations and expressions (Miller 2014; Schellekes 2017, 2019a, 2019b, 2021a). In these various primary states, where the patient's psychic movement is blocked in a way that renders their capacity for representation and working-through dormant to non-existent, the analyst's mental and emotional activeness is increased so as to retrieve and translate those parts of the patient's psyche that are waiting to be recognized, thought and formulated. In this manner, the analyst's mental and emotional activeness serves as a skilled reverberating box that listens to the sounds of the patient's psyche, especially those that are not expressed verbally or through associations.

Moreover, in these primary states, the analyst should know both how to listen to contents and how to partially ignore them when they are used as a means of escape from the aforementioned feeling of being overwhelmed or of emptiness. We are often seduced by a patient's abundant imagery and intellectual richness into overlooking or underestimating the fragile foundation that lacks the kind of stable representations capable of keeping the psyche in motion and protecting it from the extensive effects of trauma. In the absence of such representations, the analyst is often required to set aside interpretations concerning contents and fantasies, whether these interpretations are readily available or aroused by the patient, who overwhelms the analyst with a plethora of contents. Instead, the analyst should generate *bone-building interpretations* (see next chapter as well), as I propose calling the kind of interpretations that cultivate buds of a feeling/emotion/material that has emerged in the analysis but still has not been experienced by the patient; or interpretations that encompass primary anxieties of being and gradually build an alternative foundation of holding and processing where there is a prominent primary lack of such foundations in the patient's psyche. When such foundations are missing, there is a significant risk that the therapy/analysis will evolve along "pseudo-tracks" – that is to say, with more than a modicum of falseness. Thus, while both analyst and analysand may experience the analysis as good and rich, the missing foundations are ignored. Ending the analysis in this situation might, at best, create a supposedly good-enough ending or, at worst, result in a failure to reach termination in the fuller sense of the concept and instead lead to breakdown and decompensation or to the disappearance of the patient, who feels misunderstood and untouched and may or may not be able to express this feeling.

In contrast, I wish to emphasize that the opposite misstep mentioned above is also prevalent: in some cases, one grows fascinated with primary areas while obfuscating or overlooking the need to listen to higher areas in which a patient may be at a given moment. Sometimes one can see how the analyst's psyche, despite many years of study, of conducting analyses, of long-term working through, still contains at its core a primary foundation that is ruptured by primary absence or lack. At times, this foundation will exert internal pressure which seeks to connect the analyst to similar psychic states within the patient, so as to enable additional contact with the primary areas of the analyst's own psyche which have been covered over by higher developmental layers or defenses that have also formed as part of their professional development. The analyst's need to stay in touch with these primary self-nuclei acts as a magnet that seeks out similar particles in the patient's psyche. Being magnetized to, and fascinated by, the patient's primary parts may, on the one hand, increase the analyst's ability to deeply and subtly attune to these layers and, on the other hand, may often create an addiction to translating the patient's psyche on an all-too-fixed assembly line, where any psychic expression is deciphered and conceptualized as indicative of primary anxiety, even when this is not what the patient is presenting. Since clarity of expression is often limited on these primary levels, the analyst runs the risk of claiming too great a liberty in their pull towards deep and prized contact with primary areas in the patient that belong, in fact, *to their own psyche*. In such cases, blindness to, and neglect of, higher psychic levels may develop which are directly expressed by the patient (but interpreted as a defense against the deeper and more primary "real" layer) or hidden behind vague material that camouflages the more developed layers. Therefore, what may appear as an underdeveloped primary layer may serve as a defense against potential approach to material and fantasies that are present and solid in the patient's psyche, as these sometimes evoke such strong anxiety as to lead to the development of deceptive means of camouflage that take on a primary character. As mentioned, in such cases, the analyst's fascination with the primary layer might lead to a vast and dangerous misunderstanding of the patient's psyche. The image of the two parallel trains, seeking to reach the same destination but going in opposite directions, applies here as well. In such instances, the ability to reach a good-enough ending is clearly highly disrupted, given these gaps in movement and the misconstructions they entail.

A camouflaged situation of this sort occurred in an analysis with a patient who was often silent or went into extended states in which the quality of his speech was truncated, loose and vague. He felt as if he led his life enshrouded by a permanent psychic fog and gave both himself and others the impression of being formless and indistinct, to the extent that he was unable to describe any feeling or thought, no matter how basic. Given this condition, the analyst, who was skilled in listening to primary mental states and was even drawn to touching on these areas (for the above-mentioned reasons), continued to dwell in these foggy regions for long periods of time, in an attempt to fathom what the patient experienced as a very primary layer of development. It had taken quite some time to realize and discover that, for this particular patient, the vague and indistinct qualities served as a deceptive façade that had formed over many years as a protective and isolating shell/shield against being penetrated and exposed or experiencing intimacy. After the defensive function of his fogginess became apparent, what came into focus was the immense gap between the level of vagueness and the abundance of highly developed parts, fantasies, images and conflicts this patient had kept hidden under the misleading cover of obscurity. It goes without saying that this understanding enabled work of a different quality that was far more adapted to the previously hidden layers of conflict.

Fifth station: The reign of the kingdom of nostalgia

The final station I wish to address on the arduous journey towards the good-enough ending is one I call "the reign of the kingdom of nostalgia." Nostalgia, as its Greek etymology implies, is the suffering caused by the yearning to return. We all cherish, to some extent, the yearning to preserve the traces of the past, to go back to times and places in which we had experiences that we recall (or retrospectively embellish) as pleasant and valuable, to preserve the objects through which we remember our experiences with ourselves or our loved ones. This propensity enriches us with traces of our lives and with representations of past experiences and relations. However, faced with actual or felt experiences of loss which have not been sufficiently digested or mourned, the memory of the past sometimes turns into a deceptive memory, making us cling not to what actually happened but to a thing or a notion that our heart's desire insistently superimposes onto the past. In extreme situations, nostalgia can become a vicious tyrant, rigidly preserving a wonderful and idyllic past in a manner that one feels that the only way to achieve psychic peace is to return to this past or to some aspect of it. Thus, in its extreme form, nostalgia might become a magnet that keeps pulling the patient backwards, towards virtual realities that promise an illusion of calm, joy and happiness, while their present life, complex as it is, is experienced as a painful obstacle to the possibility of returning to the kingdom of the nostalgic narrative, which forces itself on the present with an emptying determination.

When nostalgia takes on qualities of daydreaming about the imagined past (Schellekes 2017, 2019b, 2021b) – for example, in statements such as: "if I could only go back to where I lived then ... if we could be in that situation now... my condition would have been entirely different" etc. – or when nostalgia grows disproportionately present, we are once again approaching the emptying out of the present. Thus, we often witness the emergence of situations in which the work of the negative and the growing prominence of negative hallucination (Green 1999) lead to experiencing what lies right in front of us as non-existent, as was so sharply expressed by Kundera: "How could she feel nostalgia when he was right in front of her? How can you suffer from the absence of a person who is present?" (Kundera 1998, p. 38).

Meanwhile, that which took place in the past gives rise to a paralyzing longing for the illusory presence of a past which, in fact, has yet to be worked through, represented and adequately mourned. This illusory dimension sustains the past as a unit that has a uniform and idyllic experiential quality, leaving the multi-layered qualities of life experiences and the traumatic aspects of actual past experiences unmetabolized, and excluding areas of experience that hold the potential to evoke pain, disappointment, doubt and confusion in order to strictly maintain the idyllic texture.[5]

Thus, metabolizing or mourning the partiality of the object or the complexity of one's experience with the object are precluded. In other words, one can view this extreme nostalgia as a camouflaged version of melancholia, though it often lacks the depressive affect and may even include a quasi-manic affect. And so, we sometimes see in therapy that the patient is already missing what is happening in the present and is, in fact, waiting for the present to become the longed-for past, while being unable to experience the present itself as having any positive actuality. Thus, neither present nor future is able to pull the patient towards either of them with their living force, serving instead as stations along a timeline, as temporal points that are wished away so that they can become past moments one can long for. Naturally, in these extreme states, reaching an ending – if it does happen – is accompanied by a tormenting yearning that keeps the patient longing for "the therapy that was" while avoiding being present in "the therapy that is," whether a good-enough one or less so.

Returning to Nathan, his psyche was far more complex than how I depicted it in the brief vignette presented above; it too was contaminated to a great extent – all too great – by a malignant nostalgia which, under the terrorism of perfection, turned any present life difficulty into a station that pushed him further away from his unmetabolized yet glorified past, to which he perhaps intended to return by taking his life.[6] His life was cut short in such a tragic manner, but the echo of his psychic layers – which he had feared so much – serves as a fruitful backdrop for this brief discussion of several stations on the Via Dolorosa of the good-enough ending, a discussion through which I hoped to touch, however lightly, its non-linear and elusive essence.

Notes

1 This chapter is reproduced here by courtesy of the *American Journal of Psychoanalysis*, where it was formerly published: Schellekes, A. (2024). Stations along the Via Dolorosa of the illusion of good-enough endings. *American Journal of Psychoanalysis, 84*: 94–110.
2 Consider, in this context, the distinction made by both Federn (1952) and Bion (1965), who note that while anyone can *feel* pain not everyone is capable of *bearing* pain in their mind, with all its weight and complexity. In other words, one must have recourse to emotional capability; moreover, there needs to exist an internal psychic space into which one could absorb painful experiences, where one could work through these experiences, reflect upon them and eventually transform poignant pain into a tolerable and metabolizable psychic experience. To the extent that these capacities are absent, when faced with psychic pain, the person will tend to evacuate it immediately, sometimes impulsively, sometimes somatically – that is to say, using any available means to keep the psyche from absorbing the painful experience into itself.
3 For a comprehensive review of this issue, see Zacharin (2021) and Salberg (2010).
4 The gamut of dynamics that lie under this emotional intensity is very large, space not permitting to detail them here. It might suffice only to mention the two extreme poles: At one end, emotions that were experienced with a past figure are transmuted/transferred on to the analyst; whereas, at the other end, the lack of intense emotions with the past figure creates a huge pressure to experience them with the analyst, occasionally for the first time, albeit in a sexualized form.
5 This line of thinking resonates with Amir's (2016) notion of the traumatic hermetic narrative, which splits existence (among other things) into a perfect pre-rupture world and total destruction post-rupture.
6 In this context, it is interesting to note Kristeva's (1989) reference to what she calls "black sun" – a pre-objectal depression within which suicide is explained as achieving a perfect union with the total and perfect object of sadness itself.

References

Aisenstein, M. & Smadja, C. (2010). Conceptual framework from the Paris psychosomatic school: A clinical psychoanalytic approach to oncology. *International Journal of Psychoanalysis*, 91: 621–640.
Amir, D. (2016). Hermetic narratives and false analysis: A unique variant of the mechanism of identification with the aggressor. *Psychoanalytic Review*, 103(4): 539–549.

Bion, W.R. (1959). Attacks on linking. *International Journal of Psychoanalysis*, 40: 308–315.

Bion, W.R. (1965). *Transformations: Change from learning to growth*. New York: Aronson, 1977.

Botella, C. & Botella, S. (2005). *The Work of Psychic Figurability: Mental States Without Representation*. Hove and New York: Brunner-Routledge.

Donnet, J.L. & Green, A. (1973). *L'enfant de ca: La Psychose Blanche*. Paris: Editions de Minuit.

Federn, P. (1952). *Ego Psychology and the Psychoses*. New York: Basic Books.

Gaddini, E. (1976). The invention of space in psychoanalysis. In *A Psychoanalytic Theory of Infantile Experience: Conceptual and Theoretical Reflections* (pp. 92–104). London: Routledge, 1992.

Gaddini, E. (1982). Early defensive fantasies and the psychoanalytical process. *International Journal of Psychoanalysis*, 63: 379–388.

Green, A. (1999). *The Work of the Negative*. London: Free Association Books.

Green, A. (2005). *Key Ideas for a Contemporary Psychoanalysis*. The New Library of Psychoanalysis. London and New York: Routledge.

Grotstein, J.S. (1990). The 'black hole' as the basic psychotic experience: Some newer psychoanalytic and neuroscience perspectives on psychosis. *Journal of the American Academy of Psychoanalysis*, 18: 29–46.

Kristeva, J. (1989). *Black Sun: Depression and Melancholia*. New York: Columbia University Press.

Kundera, M. (1998). *Identity*. London: Faber and Faber.

Marty, P. (1968). A major process of somatization: The progressive disorganization. *International Journal of Psychoanalysis*, 49: 246–249.

Miller, P. (2014). *Driving Soma – A Transformational Process in the Analytic Encounter*. London and New York: Routledge.

Salberg, J. (ed.) (2010). *Good Enough Endings: Breaks, Interruptions, and Terminations from Contemporary Relational Perspectives*. New York and London: Routledge.

Schellekes, A. (2017). Day dreaming and hypochondria – When day dreaming goes wrong and hypochondria becomes an autistic retreat. In H. Levine and D. Power (eds), *Engaging Primitive Anxieties of the Emerging Self: The Legacy of Frances Tustin*. London: Karnac.

Schellekes, A. (2019a). Arid mental landscapes and avid cravings for human contact: Beckettian and analytic narratives. *British Journal of Psychotherapy*, 35(1): 91–106.

Schellekes, A. (2019b). The dread of falling and dissolving: Further thoughts. *British Journal of Psychotherapy*, 35(3): 448–467.

Schellekes, A. (2021a). Sentenced to life: Reflections on the inability to bear vitality, following the movie "Turtles Can Fly". *British Journal of Psychotherapy*, 37(3): 493–510.

Schellekes, A. (2021b). *The Dread of Falling: Reflections on Primitive Mental States*. Tel Aviv: Resling [Hebrew].

Zacharin, R. (2021). Termination – Perhaps the end of a beginning. *Sichot*, 36(1): 39–47 [Hebrew].

Chapter 8

Concluding notes
Bone-building interpretations

In this book, I have attempted to plumb the depths of thinking about work with mental states that require us to go beyond the limits of the understanding with which we have been trained. At times, we attempt to work with extreme states – either autistic or psychotic – in which the basic psychic structure is inherently tenuous. Often, we are faced with the equally complex challenge of identifying, understanding and working with areas of lack, deprivation and absence in patients whose other parts have achieved normal or seemingly normal development; that is to say, in those who exhibit that twofold course of development I have described in the chapter "Sentenced to Life." In such a course, one part may develop to function in a relatively adaptive manner, while another part (or what lies underneath the surface) is dominated by an abyss of emptiness, uncentered-ness, disintegration anxieties and the multiple defenses mounted against these – adding up to a rigid and impenetrable structure, at one end of the spectrum, or, at the other end, a structure that is constantly overwhelmed by anxiety and lacks any clear ego boundaries.

Many of the cases presented in the book demonstrate the absence of a holding center. These uncentered mental states are analogous to the physiological state of a baby who is still incapable of sitting or holding itself upright enough to keep from falling over. In line with this analogy, I view various mental states in which a person fails to "sit upright" within themselves to such an extent as to risk experiencing potent and disintegrating primary anxieties, inescapable emptiness and the danger of fragmentation, as those of a person whose basic sensations and feelings are not known to the person themselves, whose various parts are not "glued" together, and who might experientially fall to pieces, as though they were lacking the kind of psychic pillar around which the various parts of the ego could coalesce. This person lives their life as if in constant danger of imploding into overwhelming anxiety whenever a normal level of calm cannot be maintained. The very experience of physical or psychic pain is tantamount to a catastrophe that can suck up all of existence, just like a black hole that pulls one into an intolerable void.

DOI: 10.4324/9781003479482-8

I will not go into greater detail regarding these states, as they are elaborated throughout the book. However, what I wish to highlight here is my understanding that such extreme states require a special kind of analytical presence which goes beyond containment and holding or giving meaning to nameless (Bion) or unthinkable (Winnicott) dread. I will attempt to describe some of the basic qualities of this presence as I have begun to formulate them in my mind. I hope to be able to conceptualize these more comprehensively in the future.

At this point, my emphasis is not on the kind of presence that seeks to find historical meaning and achieve mentalization – as formulated by Fonagy or, alternatively, by Levine, Mitrani and others. The ability to give meaning to, and make sense of, overwhelming physical sensations, somatic irruptions that lack all emotional context in the patient's experience, disintegration anxieties and the disappearance of parts of whatever fragile ego exists is a highly significant ability, which we strive to hone in the various states described above. Nevertheless, the layer of meaning-making cannot suffice as an initial interpretive response in such states. A structure like that which I have described in some of the book's clinical vignettes requires the analyst's highly active presence. Moreover, this presence must be of a kind capable of facilitating the growth of a much more solid psychic bone structure, compared to the patient's present state.

I am not referring either to the quality of the analyst's presence as a stable, holding, quiet and resilient counterpart who experiences within themselves the patient's most severe anxieties and is able to make meaning in those areas. In my view, this kind of presence is indeed a *sine qua non*: Its stability serves as the backdrop on whose resilient surface the patient's psyche may repeatedly project itself. This, in turn, contributes to the formation of an experience of a solid *external* structure which exists through the setting and the analyst's presence. Such an experience may be gradually internalized, at least partially, as the therapy or analysis progresses.

However, in my view, when working with psychic states that are overwhelmed by primary anxieties and the terror of internal disintegration, we must apply a more fundamental preliminary prop. One could contemplate this as something analogous to a plaster cast – a passive device required when dealing with physical fractures. The cast holds the limb or area where a bone has been fractured, immobilizing it until the body can do its job – that is, until the fracture is naturally and gradually healed. However, in my view, the stable, containing and holding presence described above, which is like a cast for fractured psychic areas – is necessary but not sufficient in the states I am addressing here. As I see it, extreme states in which a psychic support pillar has failed to emerge[1] (whether due to an innately loose ego structure, primary developmental trauma, or dramatic structural regression following later trauma) require an analytic presence which is essentially and initially also *bone-building* – meaning, an active presence which is not merely a passive external cast.

Through this image, I wish to portray a state in which the psychic skeleton is not only broken and waiting to heal but might even have failed to fully emerge, requiring active and comprehensive intervention on the part of the analyst, who strives to create the patient's interiority in the most fundamental sense – an intervention I call *"bone-building interpretation."* This type of intervention requires the analyst to first gather the fragments of the patient's experience – particles of bodily expression, manifestations of anxiety that are so void of meaning that they are experienced as particles resembling psychic gas – thus at risk of evaporating – or psychic liquid – thus at risk of spilling out (two states which leave the person with a difficult experience of having lost their self and their form). Next, these gathered particles can be marked as existing, as a primary presence in the patient's psyche. Therefore, the initial intervention in such states seeks experientially to render present and *solidify* the *event itself* – rather than its meaning, its contexts or our experience of it.

If I go back for a moment to Danny (in the chapter "The Dread of Falling"), for months on end, my role was not to offer transference interpretations or interpretations that created historical meaning or related to his patterns of relations. Rather, I had to gather and describe what was happening at a resolution that was very close to the grain of the event itself so that this description gave form to a psychic event that had not yet been experienced, or to the patient's experience of their liquid and evaporating state. For example, even a statement such as "I fell," given Danny's inability to see through his emotional eyes, was the beginning of such a bone-building interpretation. It was followed by something along the lines of: "It seems that you were very anxious in our previous session, and it's hard to see things in such a state." This kind of description may sound simplistic and overly concrete, but I wish to highlight its importance for a person who is utterly unaware of what is being experienced in these deep areas of their psyche and needs our verbalization to render their very experience robustly present. In other words, I am not simply talking about the importance of establishing an experience of a psychic bedrock or a psychic envelope – notions that have been amply addressed theoretically in psychoanalytic thinking and are imbued with sensual qualities that are calming and wrapping from the outside – but about *building* a holding and naming structure *from the inside.* Such a gradual process of building occurs through multiple interpretations that allow the patient to feel that something inside them is being gathered up into a state of solidity – not underneath their feet, as a holding floor, nor around their body, as a wrapping envelope – but something that holds the parts of the psyche as the skeletal system holds the other parts of the body.

This preliminary gathering apparently excludes the analyst as someone who feels or sees. It is obvious that no intervention can be made without the analyst being a highly perceiving and experiencing agent. However, in my understanding, the analyst's experience and presence needs to be dimmed in the states I am describing. In Danny's case, for example, making my own presence more felt at this stage would have been above and beyond what the patient was able to endure. In the third chapter, which discusses time standing still, Noga's vignette offered various examples of how many of my interventions sought to capture the parts of her experience in a manner that would result in a solid cohesiveness that was capable of linking disjointed and scattered parts of the self. As the reader may recall, Noga was a woman who lacked any sense of cohesion and would constantly photograph herself looking at herself, in a kind of endless attempt to produce a continuous and felt stable self-essence. I thus described how time after time I recalled, gathered together, sorted out, translated, connected and created links between one experience and another, one moment and another, between my reaction and hers. In that chapter, I emphasized that the range of my interventions served to slowly sew Noga's memory envelope – an envelope in which, over many years, enormous holes had formed, creating the experience that Noga was lacking an internal pillar, but was rather made up of empty holes, disjointed and meaningless segments.

I now wish to highlight another thought: When internal fragmentation is at its peak, as in Noga's case, the absence manifested in the memory envelope results from *a loose psychic skeletal structure* which is formless and at risk of fragmenting. In other words, it is *a deficiency in the vertical axis*, the axis that is supposed to link together parts of different experiences.

In what I am formulating now, I am trying to move away from the notion of psychic skin, which is ubiquitous in the writings of Bick and Anzieu, and offer an analogy which similarly draws on human anatomy but focuses on the skeletal system instead. In the context of proposing the concept of bone-building interpretations, the idea I wish to impart here concerns those kinds of presence and interventions that are capable of building that which the patient does not even feel – whether it is the absent experience of their own body parts, or their absent ability to recognize their own experiences with themselves and others. It goes without saying that work in these areas requires, in my understanding, the analyst's active mental engagement in gathering the particles of these experiences by herself and through herself. Thus, the comprehensive work I did with Danny surrounding my fall allowed me to make what had happened accessible to him piecemeal, long before such an event could be imbued with broader emotional contexts. Naturally, the process of establishing a psychic skeletal structure cannot make do with the fundamental interventions described here – they are but a cornerstone to which many more layers must be added, as happens through our analytic work.

In the states I am exploring – as manifest in Danny's emptiness and lack of a psychic spine – the lion's share of the analyst's work involves bone-building at the level of the patient's subjectivity, when the latter is either damaged or highly tenuous behind a thin façade of adaptation. When the patient's subjectivity is that tenuous, it calls for the creation of a somewhat paradoxical situation: On the one hand, the analyst must offer a highly active mental and emotional presence; on the other hand, they must apply a very potent 'dimmer' to soften their presence in the patient's experience, as it might easily overwhelm them, leading to the "toxemia of therapy" I have described. When the patient's subjectivity exists only as the experience of formless terror and annihilation, I do not see two interacting subjects – a severed, tormented psyche shaking hands with another severed and tormented psyche. Rather, I see a situation in which the analyst must minimize the presence of their own experiences and become immersed in the task of bringing the patient to meet the patient's own psychic cores.

In such a process, bone-building interpretations, which gather and nurture the primary cores of self-experience, play a significant role. These processes of gathering and entrenching subjectivity are initially performed within the analyst's psyche and only then conveyed to the patient. The way I see it, in these states the degree of relating to the other – whether through an intersubjective perspective or excessive emphasis on transference interpretations, as is sometimes common in Kleinian thinking – must be carefully regulated, as any excessive relating to another person runs the risk of pushing the patient away or detaching them from their tenuous core self.

The gamut of bone-building interpretations can be rather wide. At a basic level, it includes the analyst's effort to highlight a sensation, a basic feeling, at a certain moment, which becomes apparent to the analyst but of which the patient is completely unaware or detached from.

Later on, bone-building interpretations may gain width and depth, connecting sensations/feelings and thus gradually creating an internal evolving structure within the patient which grows in volume and density. The more this structure becomes solidified, the more the analytic work can expand to include additional analytic interventions that enable the patient to reflect on their myriad intra-psychic experiences with oneself and with another being. The expansion of such a process may take a long time, during which the analyst must find the patience required to contain frustration of whatever narcissistic needs they might have and carry the heavy load of being active in building one's mind, drop by drop, piece by piece.

Note

1 See also Pollak's work: Pollak, T. (2009). The 'body-container': A new perspective on the 'body–ego'. *International Journal of Psychoanalysis, 90*: 487–506.

Index

Note: References following "n" refer to notes.

actual neurosis, Freud's 70
actual psychosis, and relationship to blank psychosis 59
adaptation and separateness 5
adhesive equation and pseudo object relationship 46
adhesive identification 21
adhesive pseudo-object relations: and imitation 23; and sexual relations 61
aggression and denial 80
aggressor, identification with 97
"agony of consciousness" 74
Aisenstein, M. 108
Alice's Adventures in Wonderland (1996) 34
Allan, E. 35
Almond, D. 35
Alvarado, N. 36
Alvarez, A. 19
Amalia (case study) 85–87, 94–95; disconnection from self 85, 86; dream analysis 85–86; family trauma context 86; fell into episodes of depression 86; formless paintings 86; inner life oscillating between emptiness and shadowy inner reality 95; intellectual brilliance 86; psychic shutter 94; structural dissociation 87; symbiotic attachment 86; symbolization and creativity 86
analyst-assisted psychic dialysis 111
analyst's psyche, overloading of 110–111
analyst's role and challenges: addressing primary anxieties of being 112; adjusting interventions to patient's primary developmental level 111; bone-building interpretations 112; concept of figurability 111; confusion regarding patient's psychic organization 111–113; focus on cultivating emergent feelings/emotions 112; increased emotional and mental activeness of analyst 111; interpretations 112; parallel trains metaphor in analysis 113; relationship with patient's psyche 112; retrieving and translating patient's psyche 111; risk of therapy evolving along "pseudo-tracks," 112
aniconic 9n2
anti-libidinal ego 99n4
anxieties: annihilation 46; attempts to capture the moment in response to 36; body-related 70; catastrophic 5, 6, 10n5, 58, 80; death 98; development of defenses against 13; extreme unthinkable 59; hypochondriac 54, 60, 70, 72, 73, 74, 77–80; integration/non-integration 6, 95, 107; invasive 77; loss-of-self 6, 23, 25, 95; primary 95, 112; primitive 13, 30; related to mental void 57; related to time and death 37; self-observation and 70; stagnation and 96; unmentalized experiences and 60
Antoniu, M. 17
Anzieu, D. 21, 28, 76
après-coup processes 37
archaic grandiosity 18
art: and fear of dissolution 26; and loss-of-self anxiety 25; and time 34, 35–37
attachment to pain 76, 80

Auster, P. 48
autistic object 58
autistic use of rhythm as defense 62–65
aversion to life and psychic self-emptying 97

Bacon, F. 25–26
Beckett, S. 27–30; and analytic narratives
    on psychic void 53–65
behavioral patterns and traits, origins of 9
Bick, E. 7, 21
Bion, W.R. 3, 42, 57, 60, 108
Birksted-Breen, D. 37, 42
"black hole" phenomenon 57–58
blank psychosis 59
body memories 4
Bollas, C. 24
bone-building interpretations 112, 117–121
boredom and emptiness 57
Botella, C. 59, 87, 111
Botella, S. 59, 87, 111
Bowlby, J. 2

"caesura," and catastrophic anxiety 5,
    10n5
Carroll, L. 34
The Castle in the Pyrénées (1959) 26
catastrophic anxieties 58, 80; and "cae-
    sura" 5, 10n5; and developmental
    rupture 6; and gap between total self
    and limited self 6
cellular memory: and pre-conception
    phantasies 4; and retroactive
    phantasy 5
childhood dream 14
Civilization and its Discontents (1930) 44
collective unconscious 9n3
conflictual heterochrony 41
Cowan City (1993) 26
creative self 53

Dali, S. 26
Danny (patient) case study: bone-building
    interpretation; 119–120; fall in 14–15
Darboven, H. 36
David (case study) 54–57, 59–60, 61;
    abandonment and premature
    separation 56; chaos and futility in
    his life 55; collapse into terror and
    confusion 61; defense mechanisms 61;
    early life and objects 59–60; emotional
    connection and gentleness toward
    orphan kitten 56; emotional life 61;

flooding by unmentalized experiences
    60; hypochondriac anxieties 54;
    illusory sense of vitality 55; logorrhea
    and lack of self-reflection in speech
    55; negative hallucination 60;
    phantasies of rebirth and renewal 56;
    pseudo-medical interventions 60;
    rebirth phantasies 56, 60; rescue and
    recovery practices 61; rhythm of
    breakdown-recovery-breakdown 60;
    use of excitation and sensorial
    envelopes 55
daydreaming and hypochondria 69–80
daydreaming envelope 74, 76, 78, 79
excessive daydreaming 70, 75–76, 77–78
death drive and negative work (Green) 58
defensive regression and resistance to
    change 7
delusional paranoid restitution 59
denial of death and limitations 78
"dialysis machine," analyst's 110
disembodied monologue 64
The Disintegration of The Persistence of
    Memory (1952–1954) 26
disinvestment: as defense against
    unleashing instinctual chaos 59;
    destruction through 58
disobjectalizing function 58
dissolving 18–20, 22, 58, 62, 63; art and
    fear of 26; the concept of void and 57;
    self 29–30
dread of falling: as loss of mental
    balance 17; and mental collapse 13;
    negation of 14
dream: as "bizarre objects" 46;
    childhood 14; falling in 16; therapist's
    (bodily experience) 15
"dulling" of the self, Beckett's 63

early development theories, Gaddini's
    and Winnicott's views on 5
early emotional development 8, 9
early prenatal traumatic experiences 5
egoism 80
ego, under-structuralization of 62
Eigen, M. 22
emotional blindness 64, 72
emotional development, prenatal roots of 8
emotional pressure on analyst and
    patient 108
emotional versus structural mental
    void 61

emotional void 40, 55, 61
emptiness versus psychic void structures, experiences of 57–59
Eshel, O. 22
excessive rhythmicity and over-structuralization 63
The Expelled (1946) 27–30
externalization 110
extreme psychic states 109

fall 4, 13–18, 25–27
falling: absence of holding leading to 16; into black hole/void 22; as desire for dependence 18; and dissolving 30; in dreams 16; and ego psychology 17; as expression of fear of impotence 17; fear of 18, 23–26; and floating 26; and gravity 17; and loss of balance 28; meaning and symbolic expressions of 13–14; object relations theory on 18; and panic 14; symbolism 16; themes of 29; in therapeutic context 15
fantasy and transitional time 41–42
fatal psychic retreat 64
fata morgana phenomenon 1, 2
fear of being dropped (Quinodoz) 29
Ferenczi, S. 24
figurability, concept of 111
Finer, J. 36
Fishof, O. 36
flying and returning to the womb 17
fractured and fragmented time, experience of 38–40, 42–43
Freud, S. 2, 16, 37, 44, 70, 80
frozen, experience of time as 46–47
fusion-related vertigo: and annihilation anxiety 18; and being dropped 24

Gaddini, E. 2, 5–6, 21, 23, 64, 95, 107
Genesis metaphor 62
Ghobadi, B. 90
"going-on-being," Winnicott's concept of 41
Golconda (1953) 26
grandiose wishes, Eastern European folk stories on 17–18
Green, A. 23, 37, 41–42, 49, 58, 59, 63, 66n7, 108
Grotstein, J.S. 5, 7, 22, 58, 59, 66n4, 108

holding, Winnicott's concept of 16
Houzel, D. 76

human contact, dependency on 61
hypersensitivity 74
hypochondria: ambiguity in 69; auditory primal scene trauma 79; autistic features 71; autistic shell of auto-sensuality 74; castration anxiety and illness fear 79; clinical features 70; and clinical implications 77–80; confusion of suffering and pleasure 77; and contagious daydreaming 78; deficiency in splitting mechanisms 77; denial of time and aging 79; dynamics 76–77; erotic life and suffering 77; excessive daydreaming 77; Freud on 69; genesis of 77; gratification in scenarios 73; historical classification 70; imagery and emotional reality 76; imaginary catastrophes 73; internal persecutor and repressed superego 79; Iris's experience/emotional development 71–74; Kafka and 69, 80; loss of contact and control 69; masochistic component 71; medical intervention 71; negative 72, 79; obscurity in 69; personal physical symptoms 72; and psychosomatic states, clinical distinction between 70; relationship between body and emotional life 79; rich imagery of suffering 76; self-containment in 80; sexuality and 79; somatic catastrophes, daydreaming of 77; subjective experience 76–77; theoretical debates on 70; therapeutic process 73; unconscious conflictual issues 79; unconscious dynamics in 79–80
hysteria, comparison with hypochondria 70

infant's mind, in psychoanalysis 2–3
inner homeostasis, restitution of 75
instinctual drives, as semiotic signs 58
integration anxiety 6, 95, 107
internalized presence 23
internal object representations, lack of 58
internal search for lost object and hallucinatory sensory quality 59
internal void and survival, Beckett's portrayal of 63
The Interpretation of Dreams (Freud) 16
intrusive and invasive objects 81n6
invasive object 74, 81n6

Iris (patient) case study: daydreaming
73–74; hypochondriac anxieties 71–72

Kafka, F. 69, 80
Keren's therapy journey 46–47
Klein, M. 2, 22
Kundera, M. 114

libido and narcissistic regression 79
London's Institute of Contemporary Art
(ICA) 35
Longfellow, H.W. 1
Longplayer, Finer's 36
loss-of-self anxiety 6, 23, 25, 95
love and healing 80
Love of Beginnings (1993) 13
Lovesick on Nana Street (film) 23
love transference 107
Lutenberg, J.M. 61

magical omnipotent thinking 6
Magritte, R. 26, 35
Mahler, M. 2
Maiello, S. 3, 40
Mancia, M. 8
manic defense 17
Marty, P. 108
masochistic attachment to pain 80
Meantime (2000) 35
Meltzer, D. 21, 75
meaninglessness 55–56, 58, 66n4
"memoirs of the future" (Bion) 3
memory envelopes, perforated 42
mental void, concept of 57
Miller, P. 108
mirrors as symbols of object's
non-existence (Bacon) 26
Mitrani, J. 21, 22
Modell, A.H. 37
Mona's case: anxiety at entering therapy
96; emotional intensity and withdrawal 90; indirect self-therapy 96;
music session 89; self-constriction and
helplessness 96; sentenced-to-life
patient 88–90; therapeutic challenges
89; trauma and defenses 90; trauma
during adolescence 95
"More" and "Living soul" 64
motor abilities, acquisition of 16

Nathan's case 103–105, 108, 115; anxiety,
difficulty with transitions 103;

emotional functioning and coping 104;
limited self-containment and excessive
rationality 108; nostalgia and
idealization 104;; psyche contaminated
by malignant nostalgia 115; reflections
on constrained psychic capacities 105;
reflections on continuing therapy 104;
reflections on endings in analysis
and therapy 105–106; therapeutic
relationship with 103; termination 105;
negative hypochondria 72, 79
Noah (case study) 18–25; adhesive
pseudo-object relations and imitation
23; falling into black hole/void 22;
traumatic absence 23; vertigo 24
Noga (case study) 38–40, 120; adult
behavior, self-photography to capture
continuous moments 39; analytical
dynamics 38; analytical interventions
40; childhood experiences 39;
connection to family dynamics and
emotional voids 40; eating disorder
and therapeutic implications 43; food
consumption, creating continuity in
self-experience 39; fragmented
experience of time 39, 42–43; personal
background and challenges 38;
"pretend death" game 42; pretend
death as coping mechanism 39–40;
repeated descriptions of food binges 38
non-integration anxiety and fragmentation
6, 95, 107
nostalgia 113–114
"no-thingness" 57, 66n6
nothingness 54–55, 57–58, 62, 66n6
"Not I" and "Rockaby," Beckett's 63

object relations theory on falling 18
object representations, loss of 59
obsessive counting (Beckett) 27
Ogden, T. 28
Olive Green (2003) 36; video work
featuring traffic policemen eating
olives 36
omnipotent satisfaction 76
On Narcissism, Freud's 80

pain: catastrophic experience of psychic/
physical 117; of incongruity 107;
masochistic attachment to 80; and
psychic retreat 76
parental dynamics in analysis 106

patient's psychic organization, analyst's confusion regarding 111–113
perception and representation 59
perceptive amodality, in integrating sensory experiences 8
The Persistence of Memory (1931) 26
Pine, S. 37
Piontelli, A. 8
pleasure principle and reality principle 24
pleasures, through physical activity 16
Pontalis, J-B. 13
Portrait of George Dyer in a Mirror (1967–1968) 25
pre- and post-natal behaviour, continuum between 8
precocious ego development 74
prenatal life 9; facts of 10n6
"prenatal nucleus of the ego" 4
pre-representational self 8
primitive anxieties 13, 30
primitive dissociative forces 94
primitive, in psychoanalysis 1–2
primitive mental states
primitivity-maturity axis 3
proto-emotions: and primitive fears 4; and sensual womb object 3
protomental experiences 8
protomental nucleus of activity 8
pseudo-contact barrier 75
psychic abortion 61
psychic dialysis 111
psychic energy 87
psychic pain 59; and self-containment 108
psychic retreats, as refuges from human contact 29
psychic skeletal structure 120
psychic states with autistic encapsulation 46
psychic void 57–58
psychological abortion 29
psychosomatic states, comparison with hypochondria 70

Quinodoz, D. 18, 24, 26, 29

A Real Time Piece (1996) 35
rebirth phantasies, as defense against mental void 60–61
reclaiming presence, Alvarez's concept of 19
regression and transference psychosis 106
regressive states and use of rhythm 62

regressive yearnings and infantilism 96
repetitive writing and rebirth phantasy, Beckett's 65
resemblance and identicalness, losing distinction between 106–108
re-traumatization, rebirth phantasies connected with 60
reverberation time 42
rhythm of safety 60, 62
rhythms, importance/fetal experience of 40–41
"Rockaby" structure and rhythm, Beckett's 65
Rosenfeld, H. 77

schizoid retreat 29, 30
self: development of 16; dissolution of 18; hostility towards 17; and object 5, 18, 58; omnipotent 6; and other 40; reflect 25; senses of 8, 10n8
self-annihilation 108
self-dissolution, early experiences of 29–30
self-emptying 97, 108–109
sensorial maneuvers 58
separateness: adaptation and 5; annihilation and 21; frustration and 41; and fusion, oscillations between 62; partiality and 107; patient's difficulty with 7; premature 58; between self and object 107
sexual excitement and punishment, in dreams of falling 16
Slow Walk to Longplayer (2005) 36
Smadja, C. 108
smoke detector metaphor 89
somato-psychical self 8
"sound object" 3, 40
Spero, M.H. 43
Spitz, R. 2
Stern, D. 2, 8
structural mental void and emotional void 61
symbiotic links 61

Tecucianu, F. 98n2
temporal connotations 37, 41
termination of analysis 108
thin skin syndrome 88
thick skin syndrome
three-dimensional mental space 57
Three Studies of Lucian Freud (1969) 25

time: attempts to control/freeze/prolong 36–37; Bion's theory of 42; cataloguing and organizing, through dates and mathematical laws 36; context of flow 36; contrast of temporalities in analytical framework 37; developmental considerations regarding one's sense of time 40–42; dimensions in clinical setting 37–38; duration, exploration of 35; experience of fractured and fragmented time 38–40, 42–43; experience of timelessness 43–46; fetal development and 41; as frozen, ritualistic, stereotypic 46–47; as metaphor for inner reality 34; representations of personal and social 36; reverberation 42; subjective experience of 34; symbolism in art as means to decipher and capture time's conflicting 34; works of art and 35–37; see also Yoav's sense of time/experience of timelessness
timeless modality 78
"time she stopped" and "rock her off" 64
Time Transfixed (1938) 35
toxemia of therapy 89, 97, 98, 108–110, 121
transference: love 107; and prenatal dynamics 4; and regression 7; in therapy 106
transitional time 42
trauma 26, 59–60, 64, 87, 93, 97; and adolescence 88; auditory primal scene experiences 79; cumulative 96; and death anxiety 98; and defences 90; difficulty in compartmentalizing 95; effects on psychic motion and stability 111; and emotional excess 94; and emotional impact 89; internal turbulence and life-sustaining ability 85; and its impact 92; and loss 94; primary and late-onset 85; primitive mental states and 111–112; re-traumatization 60, 75, 98; time as metaphor for 35; time dimensions in 88; and vitality 85, 87; and waiting 42
traumatic absence 23
Travels in the Scriptorium (2006) 48
Trevarthen, C. 2
Triptych May-June 1973 25
Turtles Can Fly 85, 88, 90–94, 96–97
Tustin, F. 2, 13, 18, 21, 22, 24, 30, 58, 74
Twilight in the Nursery (1990) 35

unbearable human experiences, expression of 53
uncentered mental states 117
unconscious processes, concept of 44
universal memory preconceptions 3

veil of sexual maturity covering primary needs 108
vertigo 18, 24
visual metaphors and disembodiment, Beckett's 63
vitality: and aliveness 87, 90; and dead life 94; and death 90, 91; in psychotherapy and analysis 85; theoretical meaning of 99n3; analyst's capacity to bear 97; and trauma 85, 87; and unbearable emptiness 87
"voice from the crypt," Grotstein's concept of 7
void, concept of 57
void existence, in "Rockaby" 65
void states, of mind 22, 53–54, 57–58, 60–65

Wilheim, J. 5
Williams, G. 75
Williams, P. 81n6
Winnicott, D.W. 2, 5, 16, 17, 23, 25, 41, 58, 76
work as "consecrated to the void," concept of (Beckett) 57
writer's immersion and expression 53
writing as structuring experience 53
Writing Time (Darboven) 36

Yerka, J. 26, 35
Yoav's sense of time/experience of timelessness 43–46; blurring memory traces, especially pain of loss 45; contrast with Noga's fragmented memory 45; denial of past, trauma, and future death 44; link to depression and death anxiety 44; manic defense against loss and death 44; pleasure in sensation of everlasting present 43–44; sense of déjà vu as defense against death anxiety 45; separation and death anxiety 45; tension between déjà vu and jamais vu experience 45

For Product Safety Concerns and Information please contact our EU
representative GPSR@taylorandfrancis.com
Taylor & Francis Verlag GmbH, Kaufingerstraße 24, 80331 München, Germany

www.ingramcontent.com/pod-product-compliance
Lightning Source LLC
Chambersburg PA
CBHW070347270326
41926CB00017B/4031

9 781032 758718